INSIGHT COMPACT GUIDE

MOSCOW

Compact Guide: Moscow is the ultimate easy-reference guide to the Russian capital. It tells you everything you need to know about Moscow's great attractions, from St Basil's Cathedral to the Bolshoi Theatre, from the Kremlin to the Tretiakov Gallery.

This is one of 130 Compact Guides produced by the editors of Insight Guides, whose books have set the standard for visual travel guides since 1970. Packed with information, arranged in easy-to-follow routes, and lavishly illustrated with photographs, this book not only steers you round Moscow but also gives you fascinating insights into local life.

GW00482951

APA PUBLICATIONS
Part of the Langenscheidt Publishing Group

Star Attractions

An instant reference to some of Moscow's most popular tourist attractions to help you on your way.

Kremlin p16

Cathedral of the Assumption p21

Ivan the Great Bell Tower p22

State Armoury p25

Red Square p27

St Basil's Cathedral p29

Church of the Trinity in Nikitniki p32

St Sergius Monastery p74

Bolshoi Theatre p36

Tretiakov Gallery p57

Introduction

Places

Culture

Leisure

Practical Information

Moscow – The Heart of Russia

With a population of around 10 million inhabitants, Moscow (Moskva) – ranks as one of the biggest cities in the world. Although Peter the Great demoted the city from its rank of Tsar's capital in favour of the more European St Petersburg, Moscow always remained the heartland capital of the Russian people. Home for Pushkin, Lermontov and Dostoyevsky, it became a breeding ground for progressive thought and a haven for free-thinkers.

After Lenin and the Bolsheviks seized power in the October Revolution of 1917, Moscow's capital city status was restored. As capital of the former USSR, it was by far the most important city in the vast Soviet empire, which collapsed after the failed *coup d'état* of 1991. For 70 years it served as the administrative, economic, cultural and religious centre for the whole communist structure as well as the capital of the Russian republic. Now, as then, Moscow occupies a pivotal position as the link between two worlds – the East and the West.

Moscow still leads the nation in research, the sciences, intellectual life, education and training. The Presidium of the Academies of Science, Medicine, Pedagogy, Technology, Agriculture and Construction are all based in Moscow. Many of the leading figures in these prestigious institutions now enjoy a worldwide reputation. More than 25,000 students are enrolled in Moscow's Lomonosov University (MGU). Although many private universities and colleges have opened in the last few years, MGU's diploma is still the most valued. The city runs 2,000 libraries, including the Russian National Library, 350 museums, many laboratories and research institutes as well as schools, technical colleges and polytechnics.

After the fall of the Soviet Union, Moscow soon became one of the world's major tourist cities. Tour groups and study programs were filled by people curious to get a glimpse behind the old Iron Curtain. They were soon joined by foreign businessmen who were keen to capitalise on the country's emerging markets. Now the city is truly cosmopolitan – and cultured. Theatre performances and concerts are nearly always sold out and museums attract western tourists.

Moscow today is a vibrant city, enjoying a lively nightlife. The soviet past has not been completely forgotten though, and still makes itself felt in any number of ways. Though each year the queue for Lenin's Mausoleum grows shorter; and if you see a long line on Tverskaya Ulitsa, it's not going to be for bread. More likely it's Moscow's younger generation patiently waiting for a seat in a trendy restaurant or the latest imported fashion.

Casting a ballot for the future

View from Moskvoretsky Bridge

Location and size

The European part of Russia is a continuation of the East European Plain which rises to the Central Russian Uplands north of the Donets basin. Further to the east, the Ural mountains form a natural dividing line between European and Asian Russia with the West Siberian Plain, Central Siberian Plateau and East Siberian Mountains beyond. Russia is bordered to the south by the foothills of the Caucasus Mountains, the waters of the Black Sea and the Caspian Sea and the steppes of Kazakhstan and Mongolia. In the far east, the River Amur forms the border with China. In the west, the rivers flow in a north-south direction, while in the Asian part they normally flow from south to north.

Moscow lies on a hilly plain 142m (450ft) above sea level with a typical continental climate. The area of the city is over 1,000sq km (390sq miles) making it one of the biggest cities in the world. The 109km (68 mile) urban motorway ring encircles Greater Moscow and its diameter ranges from 35–40km (22–25 miles). But the city's conurbation now extends well beyond the motorway.

The River Moskva flows through the city from northwest to southeast and its width varies from 150–200m (450–600ft). Its biggest tributary, the Yauza, joins the Moskva from the northeast, necessitating the 40 bridges that span the two rivers inside the city boundaries. A navigable canal links the Moskva with the Volga and an extensive system of waterways connects Moscow with the Black Sea, the Caspian Sea, the Sea of Azov, the White Sea and the Baltic.

Belorussian Station

With its central location, Moscow is also the country's major terminal for road, rail, river and international flights. The main approach roads into the city, important trade routes even in the Middle Ages, link into the concentric pattern of the city's road network. The main railway lines approach the city centre in a similar way.

The Russian climate

The influence of the Atlantic Gulf Stream tails off from west to east, so that the vast, flat plains enjoy a typical continental climate with hot, dry summers but extremely cold winters. The regions in the far north which are surrounded by frozen sea for nine months of the year hardly experience a summer at all.

In southern Siberia, it lasts from June to September. Only the region around the Black Sea enjoys a mild, subtropical climate. About 10 million sq km (3.8 million sq miles) or 46 percent of the surface area, mainly in the north and east, is subject to permafrost conditions.

Moscow is in the temperate continental climatic zone. Summer lasts from mid-May to the end of August and

Moscow's annual rainfall is low

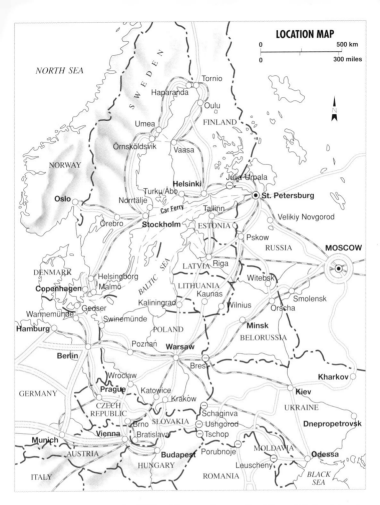

LOCATION MAP

0   500 km

0   300 miles

the average temperature is 18°C, with a maximum of around 30°C. In the winter months, snow falls from the end of December, and the temperatures can fall as low as –30°C. The city's annual rainfall is only 575mm (22in).

Politics and economy

The politics of modern Russia began with the fall of the Soviet Empire. Only when Mikhail Gorbachev, the Secretary General of the Communist Party and later president from 1985–91, set about reforming the fossilised political structure with policies of *glasnost* (openness) and *perestroika* (restructuring) were its weaknesses made clear. The rest of the world responded with more than just curiosity as he attempted to persuade the communist bureaucrats to abandon their old ways. The process of change

Moscow's industrial centre

gathered pace with the policies of market reform pursued under Boris Yeltsin, who became president of the Russian Federation in 1992.

The Yeltsin years were characterised by a chaos that seemed to emanate from the shambling figure of the President himself. The country was awash with overt bribery and corruption, and this became a part of everyday life, accepted with the same resignation as, say, a missed bus. Yeltsin launched the first Chechen War, some say whilst drunk, needing as he reportedly said, 'A small victorious war,' to boost his popularity before elections in 1996. He was elected for a second term and heavily favoured by Western leaders who were afraid for investments – both current and future, if the Communists in the form of Gennady Zuganov returned to power. Nevertheless, the country lurched towards an economic crisis in 1998, which wiped out the country's burgeoning middle class at a stroke. Suddenly, Yeltsin's ability to stabilise the chaotic country was cast into doubt at home and abroad. On New Year's Eve 1999, Yelstin handed over power to the little known Vladimir Putin, and the country, as well as investors, breathed a sigh of relief. It wasn't just that they disagreed with Yeltsin's policies: many Russians, whilst traveling abroad for perhaps the first time in their lives, felt ashamed of the image that Yeltsin was giving of their homeland. Putin, an ex-KGB man, German speaker, and almost teetotaller, promised something else at least.

President Putin's rule has been characterised by an increase in the power of the security forces, *Silovki*, and by state interference in the economy, especially against the rising number of rich and powerful oligarchs (Moscow boasts more billionaires than any other city in the world).

Moscow has become a sophisticated consumer capital

Yukos, one of the nation's largest oil companies, was hounded through the courts, and their owner Mikhail Khodorkovsky was arrested in 2003, for apparently disregarding an agreement made between politicians and the oligarchs that the latter could keep their wealth, obtained through rigged state auctions in the early 1990s, in exchange for a policy not to take part in political life. Khodorkovsky, who began funding Putin's opponents in the December 2003 parliamentary elections, subsequently felt the full force of the President's wrath. However, such dramas are of little concern to the average Russian, being as it is essentially a battle between two rival clans.

Harvest in the farmlands

Putin was reelected in 2004 when he gained 70 percent of the vote, despite failing to offer any programme or plans for the future. (The fact that he had no realistic opponents also helped, of course.)

Of more concern is the ongoing Chechen War, which is increasingly making itself felt in Moscow and other cities of the Russian Federation. The Moscow metro has been bombed, planes blown up, theatres attacked, and then, in September 2004, over 350 Russians, many of them children, perished when terrorists seized a school in the small North Ossetian city of Beslan.

9

In 2005 subsidised medicine and travel for the country's worst off were cancelled, in favour of a system of payments. However, many people felt that these payments were either too small, or would not be paid at all by the cash-strapped local authorities, and demonstrations, the largest since 1991, mainly attended by pensioners, broke out across the country.

Pensions were raised, and in Moscow the authorities eventually relented, providing subsidised travel and medicine out of the state budget. However, in the regions where the local authorities lack such funds, protests continued, and, as of this printing, the situation has yet to be resolved.

This discrepancy between Moscow and the rest of the country (excluding St Petersburg) is one of the most striking features of life in Russia today. Salaries are anything up to 10 times higher in Moscow, and, as a result, people flock to the capital. However, until recently, non-Muscovites were required to obtain registration in order to stay in Moscow for more than three days, registration that was difficult and expensive to maintain. This system was altered at the end of 2004, and the term extended to three months. Despite this, possibly temporary, relaxation of the rules, there remains a vast gulf between Moscow and other regions.

People

Moscow is a melting pot of faces, languages, accents and religions. Russians form the traditional majority, but there are many Ukrainians, Tatars, Armenians, Jews, Georgians

Happy days ahead?

and Belorussians. There are now about ten million people living in Moscow. Every day Moscow has up to three million visitors and up to five million on public holidays. Were it not for the resident permit system, the population might easily double. This is nothing to do with natural increment (most families are small, having only one child or no children) but everything to do with the migration of out-of-town manpower because, in the minds of millions of people – particularly the young – the myth that 'you have to leave your hole and go to Moscow to see some real life' predominates. And yet there are more pensioners in Moscow than workers – between two and three million of them. In terms of average age, Moscow is is the oldest capital in the world. These old men and women eke out an existence on a tiny pension with no one to care for them. Although regularly increased, this pension never really covers anything but the very basics. In contrast, rich people make up only five percent of the population and enjoy a very luxurious life-style.

In Soviet times almost all housing was state-owned and some people lived in communal flats in which they shared the kitchen and bathroom with other families. At the beginning of the reforms these were sold into private hands by the municipal authorities. Mortgages are slowly becoming easier to obtain, and many Muscovites have taken the opportunity. For non-Muscovites, however, without Moscow registration, buying a flat is as hard as ever.

Owning a decent car, however, is no longer a problem: there is a plentiful supply of Russian and imported cars, both new and second-hand. Many families own one or two cars and the fuel lines familiar at the beginning of *perestroika* have disappeared. Now the biggest problem for car owners is finding a place to park, although the Moscow government is promoting a special programme for the construction of new garages and parking places. As in many other cities, traffic jams have also become a nightmare.

Although Muscovites tend to be brusque on the street, they are a very hospitable people: when you visit them at home, the entire contents of their refrigerators will be spread out on the table. Still, this type of behaviour is more normal for the older generation. Young people have been influenced by western culture and are likely to be more neutral in their behaviour.

Language

More than 150 languages are spoken in Russia, but nearly all of the 147 million inhabitants of the former Soviet republics can speak Russian to some degree. Russian, along with the Ukrainian and Belorussian languages, belongs to the East Slavic languages. The Cyrillic script developed from Old Shurch Slavonic, which was based on the Greek script.

10

Mongolians, a small minority in Moscow

Russian uses the Cyrillic script

Historical Highlights

The region around the Moskva, Volga and Oka rivers was inhabited from pre-historic times by people who lived by hunting and fishing. They settled in the dense forest and used the rivers as their link with the outside world.

Swedish Varangians or Vikings crossed the Baltic and advanced southwest along the rivers setting up fortified trading settlements along the banks. Under the leadership of the legendary Rurik who had Byzantium in his sights, the Varangians established strongholds in Novgorod and Kiev. They mixed with the indigenous Rus population and created the first two Russian principalities in the north and south around these centres.

1147 The Prince of Suzdal, Yury Dolgorukiy invites his ally Prince Sviatoslav Olgovich of Novgorod to Moscow. This event is the first documented mention of Moscow. Recent archaeological excavations have unearthed evidence that at the end of the 11th century a settlement existed where the River Neglinnaya meets the Moskva around the Borovitsky hill in what is now the Kremlin.

1156 Yury Dolgorukiy builds a defensive palisade around the Kremlin hill, covering an area equal to about one twentieth of the present-day Kremlin. It provides the inhabitants of the surrounding area, including craftsmen and merchants, with protection from attack.

1238 Batu Khan, grandson of Genghis Khan, conquers Moscow and for the next 250 years until 1480 compels the Russian princes to pay tribute to the Golden Hordes (Mongols).

Towards the end of the 13th century the city, under the domination of the Mongolian hordes, becomes the capital of the principality of Moscow and gains in importance over ther towns of the principality of Vladimir-Suzdal.

1328 Ivan Kalita or 'Money Bags' is made Grand Prince by the Khan. He moves his residence from Vladimir to Moscow, where he sets about constructing his kremlin – a fortress – built from sturdy oak trees.

The first stone buildings, churches and living accommodation, are constructed inside the walls. Around 30,000 people live in the city and a number of fortified monasteries are built at the entrances to the city. To the east of the Kremlin walls, the trading and artisan centre later to become known as Kitay-Gorod, develops into a sizeable district.

1368 Dmitry Ivanovich (Donskoy) extends the Kremlin with a new stone wall, which withstands two sieges by the Mongols.

1380 Grand Prince Dmitry defeats the Mongols in the Battle of Kulikovo on the Don. To avenge their defeat, the Mongols lay siege to Moscow two years later and burn it to the ground. Nevertheless the city soon recovers and becomes a symbol of Russian unity.

c 1400 The influence of the Golden Horde's yoke begins to wane. The now wealthy monasteries and boyars (nobles) enjoy prosperity and the first Russian artists, such as Feofan Grek (Theophanes the Greek), Andrei Rublev and Daniil Chyorny establish themselves.

1462–1505 Ivan III completes the unification of the lands around Moscow. He calls himself the 'Grand Prince of Moscow and All Russia' and marries Zoe Paleolog, the niece of Constantine XII, the last emperor of Byzantium, who had been defeated by the Muslim Ottomans in 1453. Russia now succeeds Byzantium as the 'second Rome'.

At a time when the Renaissance was gaining ground in western Europe, Ivan summons architects and artists, mainly from Italy, but also from the historic Russian cities of Pskov, Vladimir and Novgorod, to give the city the splendour worthy of a 'third Rome'. The period sees the rebuilding of the Cathedral of the Assumption and the construction of the equally beautiful Annunciation and Archangel cathedrals. The Kremlin is rebuilt in stone, as ironworks, foundries and studios are constructed along western European lines, trade links are developed and diplomatic relations with the rest of Europe established. The population increases to 100,000 and the area of the city now covers 5.4sq km (2sq miles). Moscow is one of the biggest cities in the world.

1538 The earth mound which surrounds Kitay-Gorod, the district to the northeast of the Kremlin and home to craftsmen and merchants, is replaced by a brick wall.

1547 Two fires engulf much of the town.

1547–84 Ivan IV, or Ivan the Terrible, is crowned Tsar of All Russia. He defeats the Tartars in Kazan and Astrakhan. He commissions more new buildings in Moscow.

1563 Moscow's first printed book appears.

c 1600 Boris Godunov builds another wall, which encircles the entire Kremlin and Kitay-Gorod in a horse-shoe shape.

The new parts of the city are named Belgorod (White City), as its inhabitants were relieved (whitened) of paying certain taxes. These walls remained until the 19th century, when they were finally demolished to make way for the Boulevard Ring. An additional, fourth concentric wall is built. This is now occupied by the Garden (Sadovoye) Ring. The newly created district is named Zemlyanoy Gorod.

Beyond the ramparts to the south and east, a chain of strongly fortified monasteries is established, including the Novodevichy and Danilov convents. Improved security allows trade and craft manufacture to flourish, with different quarters being occupied by different trades. The market in Red Square between the Kremlin and Kitay-Gorod emerges as the centre of commercial activity.

1612 Minin and Posharsky liberate Moscow from the Poles and Lithuanians who occupied the city in 1610. 15 years later, the city which had been destroyed in the battles, is fully restored. Under the Romanov dynasty, which dates from 1613, cloth, paper, brick and glass making factories are introduced. The carillon in the Spasskaya (Saviour) Bell Tower rings out over a city of 200,000 inhabitants.

1633 Moscow's first water main is built.

1671 Stepan Razin, now something of a folk-hero, leads an uprising of peasants in the Volga and Don regions and is later executed in Moscow as a warning to the inhabitants.

1689–1725 Peter the Great carries out a number of domestic reforms, including laws to improve sanitation, construction and the highways and also a system of recruits for regular army service.

After 1703, many officials, noblemen and clerics move to St Petersburg, and even though the 'head' of government leaves for St Petersburg in 1713, the 'heart' of Russia remains in Moscow. Many new industries are established in the city.

1755 Mikhail Lomonosov founds the city's first university. It is at around this time that architects such as Giacomo Quarenghi and Vasily Stasov begin to leave their splendid mark on the city.

1773 The contrast between the luxurious residences of the aristocrats and the abject misery of the poor who are still living in wooden huts is just as apparent in Moscow as in the rest of Russia and it is what lies behind the peasants' uprising initiated by the Cossack Pugachov. He represents some hope of relief from unremitting misery, but the uprising is put down by troops, Pugachov is captured, brought to Moscow in chains and publicly executed.

1786 On the edge of the city, a relief canal is dug parallel to the River Moskva, creating an island south of the Kremlin.

1787 Work starts on a water main to provide a regular supply of drinking water.

1812 Napoleon invades Russia and after defeating Russian forces at the Battle of Borodino, he occupies Moscow. Fire destroys two-thirds of the houses. Disruption of supplies by the partisans, hunger and continuing harassment from the Russian army force Napoleon to withdraw.

1813 The Commission for the Construction of the City of Moscow is set up, and a programme of rebuilding is launched. The Kremlin Great Palace, the Armoury and the Riding School are built.

1816 Secret societies, such as the aristocratic revolutionaries known as Decembrists, are established with the aim of abolishing serfdom.

1825 The Bolshoi Theatre is re-opened after a fire in 1805 destroyed the first building. The Decembrist Rising is crushed by Nicholas I.

1851 Railway between Moscow and St Petersburg is opened.

1861 The abolition of serfdom is followed by a huge influx of landless peasants to the cities. By the end of the 19th century, Moscow's population has risen to one million.

1866 The Moscow Conservatory is opened.

1890 Electric trams are introduced.

1905 Moscow workers rise up against tsarism and the bourgeoisie. The October strike and the armed uprising in December by Moscow workers force the tsar to accept a parliament with limited powers.

1914 Russia enters World War I against Germany, but it brings untold misery to Muscovites.

1917 On 28 February, a second uprising wins the support of most Muscovites who want to see an end to tsarist rule. On 25 October (or 7 November), the socialist revolution sees the Bolsheviks under Lenin take power in St Petersburg.

1918 Moscow becomes capital of Soviet Russia.

1920 By the end of the civil war, the devastated city's population has fallen to one million.

1922 Foreign troops leave Russian soil. Lenin declares the Union of Soviet Socialist Republics and Moscow is named as its official capital.

1924 Lenin dies. Petrograd is renamed Leningrad.

1926 The population rises to two million and the first five-year modernisation plan is implemented.

1933 Trolleybuses are introduced.

1935 A General Plan for the Development of Moscow along the lines of the old road system is drawn up. The ring and radial roads are to be retained, while the banks of the Moskva are to be reinforced with granite. New bridges and a canal linking the Moskva with the Volga are planned. An 11km (6 mile) stretch of underground railway opens.

1941 Germany invades Russia. In October and November, two German offensives against Moscow are brought to a halt. In December, a Russian counter attack forces the Germans to withdraw.

1945 On 9 May, the Russians celebrate victory and the end of the war.

1947 The underground network is extended, and a new programme of domestic housing and administrative buildings is started.

1956 The XX Communist Party Congress exposes Stalin's personality cult, restores civil rights and rehabilitates millions of innocent Soviet citizens.

1961 On 14 April, Moscow honours the first Russian cosmonaut Yuri Gagarin. The motorway around Moscow is completed and the Palace of Congresses is opened in the Kremlin.

1971 A new General Plan for the Development of Moscow comes into force.

1980 Moscow hosts the XXII Olympiad. Second international airport opens at Sheremetyevo.

1986 The XXVII Communist Party Congress agrees to a period of democratisation characterised by the policies of *glasnost* (openness) and *perestroika* (restructuring). The youthful party leadership under Mikhail Gorbachev catches the mood of the Soviet people, who are keen to see change.

1991 A failed coup d'état by hardline communists leads to the demise of Gorbachev, the collapse of communism and the disintegration of the USSR. The Commonwealth of Independent States takes its place under the leadership of Boris Yeltsin.

1993 Yeltsin wins nationwide referendum. In July the hardliners roll back on reforms, leading the president to dissolve the parliament in September and call new elections for December. The hardliners occupy the parliament building until October 4, when Yeltsin sends in the tanks to force their surrender. After the December elections – the first freely held elections since 1917 – the nationalist Liberal Democrats emerge as a formidable force.

1994 The Russians attack Grozny, the Chechen capital beginning what they call the First Chechen War. Tens of thousands die or flee their homes.

1996 Yeltsin wins presidential election.

1997 Moscow celebrates its 850th anniversary.

1999 Yeltsin hands over power to Vladimir Putin in a live TV broadcast on New Year's Eve.

2004 Vladimir Putin wins reelection with a landslide majority.

2006 Moscow hosts key meetings of the G8, during the year of its presidency. Plans to complete Catherine the Great's Tsartisyno estate are revealed.

Route 1

★★★ The Kremlin

From a commanding position overlooking the Moskva, the Kremlin stands in the centre of Moscow and at the heart of Russia. Although the buildings which form the Kremlin date from different periods in Russian history, there is a distinct unity of style. An old Russian proverb says: The Kremlin stands above Moscow, but only heaven stands above the Kremlin.

History

Yury Dolgorukiy is regarded as the founder, when in 1156 he built a palisade around a thickly wooded hill. He set up his camp within this fence, which was later re-

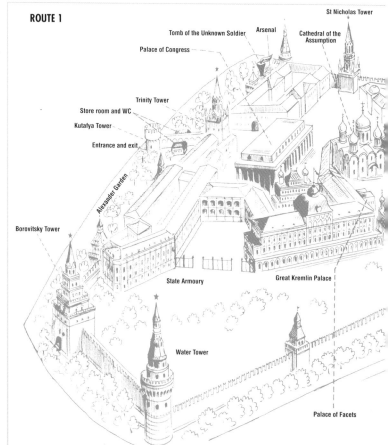

ROUTE 1

St Nicholas Tower

Tomb of the Unknown Soldier
Arsenal
Cathedral of the Assumption

Palace of Congress

Trinity Tower

Store room and WC

Kutafya Tower

Entrance and exit

Alexander Garden

Borovitsky Tower

State Armoury

Great Kremlin Palace

Water Tower

Palace of Facets

placed by an oak palisade. Dmitry Ivanovich (Donskoy) built a stone wall in 1367.

Very little of these early fortifications remain. The 2,235m (2,445 yd) wall with twenty towers and gates covers a triangular surface area of 28 hectares (70 acres).

The Kremlin is bordered to the west by Borovitsky Square, to the east by Red Square and to the southeast by the River Moskva. In some places the wall can reach 20m (62ft) in height and 8m (25ft) in width.

View from the river

Like most other fortifications in old Russian cities, the Kremlin was originally built to defend the town and its inhabitants. Many changes have taken place over the centuries reflecting the long history of the city. After the assaults by the Tartars and Mongols, the fortifications were deemed necessary as a protection against the increasing danger from outsiders. Contrary to the defensive strat-

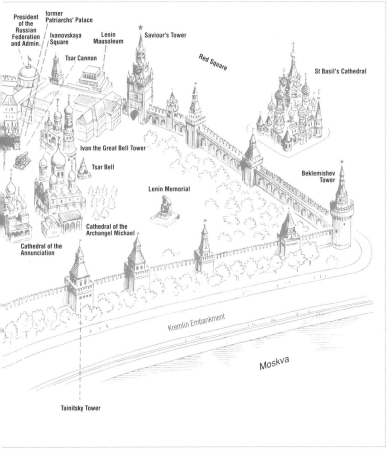

egy of the time, the Kremlin was built with not one, but four gates. These gave the population in the outlying villages the chance to seek shelter behind the walls if an attack was imminent.

Under Ivan III (1462–1505), the Kremlin became the seat of government for the now independent tsars and the spiritual leaders or patriarchs of the Russian Orthodox church. Foreign architects were summoned to Moscow to redesign the wall in Renaissance style and to build cathedrals and palaces which reflected the power and dignity of the strongest state in eastern Europe.

During the 16th and 17th centuries, as the tsars extended their empire beyond Moscow, west European and Russian architects were creating a collection of buildings which now uniquely document the cultural and artistic development of the city.

In 1713, Moscow lost its capital city status to St Petersburg, and in the first half of the 18th century, new building was restricted to military installations. In the second half of the century, however, Catherine the Great commissioned the Senate in Classical style and the Grand Kremlin Palace was built by Nicolas I in the first half of the 19th century.

In March 1918, Moscow resumed its position as capital of Russia and the Kremlin, with its special significance to the Russian people, became the seat of government for the new Soviet Republic.

In the 1930s, work started on transforming the old royal and patriarchal residences into the administrative headquarters of a Soviet government only too well aware of its own international mission. Some of the monasteries and

State cars in Kremlin Square

Former Government building

churches were demolished, secular buildings were converted for official use, but the cathedrals were restored and well cared for. In 1937, the main entrances and towers were topped by five-pointed stars made of ruby glass which still turn in the wind and are illuminated at night.

A team of architects designed the marble and glass Palace of Congresses in 1961. The Communist Party Conference was held there in the October of the same year.

After World War II, the Kremlin was opened to members of the public.

Sightseeing

A walk around the outside of the Kremlin wall will give an indication of the size of the citadel, although the views from the Moskva Bridge or from Red Square are equally impressive. The distance around the external walls is 2.5km (1½ miles).

The nearest Metro stations to the Kremlin are *Borovitskaya/Biblioteka imeni Lenina*, *Alexandrovsky Sad* and *Arbatskaya*. A tour of the Kremlin starts at the Troitskaya (Trinity) Gate, the only public entrance, which is reached through the Alexander Gardens (Friday–Wednesday 10am–6pm, last tickets 5.30pm; closed the first Saturday of the month; tickets can be bought at the kiosk by the gate). The following descriptions cover only the buildings which are of special interest.

The Trinity Tower

Debating the issues

The **Trinity Tower**, the highest of the Kremlin towers, is a counterpoint to the Saviour's Tower, the Kremlin's principal gateway. It was built in 1495 and consists of seven storeys and a number of cellars which were used as ammunition stores. Only a few yards beyond it stands the **Palace of Congresses** (Dvorets Syezdov), which was built at the beginning of the 1960s under the direction of architect Posokhin. It took 15 months to complete and at the time its design which employed glass, concrete, aluminium and marble was regarded as innovative. It was used for political meetings, but now hosts conferences, opera and rock concerts, and performances by the Bolshoi theatre company. With accommodation for 6,000 people, it has excellent acoustics and a superbly equipped stage. Escalators lead up to a splendid banqueting hall with accommodation for 2,500. Every year, the rooms of the Palace of Congresses are opened up to the children of Moscow for New Year festivities, with Christmas trees and 'Father Frost'.

To the left of the Palace of Congresses is the long, narrow **Arsenal**. It was built for Peter the Great by architects Mikhail Cheglokov, Dmitry Ivanov and the German Christoph Konrad. Its straightforward neoclassical style matches the function for which it was originally intended, even though at one time there were plans to turn it into an army museum. The baroque portico is the work of

Arsenal, built for Peter the Great

The Russian flag

The 40-tonnes Tsar Cannon

The 221-tonnes Tsar Bell

Ukhtomsky. The cannon in front of the east wall were captured from the French during the Napoleonic wars in 1812.

To the right is the triangular Senate. Built in Classical style for Catherine the Great between 1771–85 by Kazakov, it used to house the Russian Government. The red hammer and sickle flag of the old USSR has disappeared from above the green dome on the former Council of Ministers building and it is now the white, blue and red flag of Russia which flies from the flagpole.

The building is not open to the public, but may be visited by politicians, researchers and guests of the nation. It housed the Council of Commissars, the Defence Council and the Politburo of the Communist Party and a narrow passageway leads into the living room of the flat where Lenin lived with his wife Nadezhda Krupskaya and his sister Mariya Ulyanova.

Directly behind the former Senate building is the **Presidential Administration** (formerly USSR), which with its yellowy-white walls, green roof, portico and facade looks as though it too dates from the reign of Catherine the Great. Yet it was in fact built between 1932–4 by von Röhrberg on the site of the Small Nicholas Palais and an old monastery. At the moment it is the official residence of the President of the Russian Federation. In 1958, the Kremlin Theatre was opened in Röhrberg's building.

To the west of the **Presidential Administration** is Kremlin Square, formerly Ivanovskaya Square and here at the southern end beside the Tainitsky garden stands the Lenin Monument by the contemporary sculptor Pinchuk. On the right side of Kremlin Square is the **Tsar Cannon** (Tsar Pushka). This huge cannon, cast in bronze in 1586 by Andrei Chokov, was never fired. It weighs 40 tonnes, and with a calibre of 890mm (35ins), measures 5.35m (17ft) in length.

Raised on a special pedestal, only a few yards from the Tsar Cannon stands the **Tsar Bell** (Tsar Kolokol). It is 6.14m (20ft) high, weighs 210 tonnes and it was cast by Ivan and Mikhail Motorin between 1733–5. It is decorated in elaborate relief with portraits of the second Romanov Tsar Aleksei Mikhailovich and the Empress Anna Ivanovna. Even a small section of the bell which broke off in a fire weighs 11 tonnes. It can be seen lying near the granite plinth.

The ★★ **Cathedral Square** (Sobornaya Ploschad) was laid out in the 15th century and has for centuries been regarded as the heart of the Kremlin. It is bordered to the north by the Cathedral of the Dormition (also called the Cathedral of the Assumption), to the west by the Palace of Facets and one side of the Great Kremlin Palace, to the south by the Cathedral of the Annunciation and to the east by the bell tower of Ivan the Great.

The ★★★ **Cathedral of the Assumption** (Uspensky Sobor), the largest church in the Kremlin, was commissioned by Ivan III from the Italian architect Aristotle Fioravanti and was built between 1475–9 on the site of Ivan Kalita's wooden church of the same name. The architects used the Church of the Assumption in Vladimir, which was built between 1185–9, as their model and many features, including the five gilt domes, roof arcades, window recesses and portals, are similar. In addition, Fioravanti introduced new architectural forms of the Italian Renaissance, which were later adopted by Russian ecclesiastical architecture. This blend of east and west characterises the architectural developments during the reign of Ivan III.

Distinctive gilt domes and roof arcades

Enter the cathedral from the western entrance. The original frescoes on the walls and the four round piers are the work of the Russian painter Dionisy, but were extensively renovated in the 1950s. In the east, the iconostasis separates the sanctuary from the nave. The most famous icons on the screen include St George (12th-century and pure Byzantine), the Virgin of Vladimir, the Saviour with the Fiery Eye and Old Testament Trinity (14th-century).

Detail of fresco by Dionisy

From 1547 to 1894, the Grand Prince was crowned as Tsar of All Russia here and the throne of Ivan the Terrible (1551) and of Aleksei Mikhailovich (1645–76) as well as the patriarch's chair are reminders of these occasions.

21

In September 1990, the cathedral, which was used as a museum during the Soviet period, was given back to the Russian Orthodox church and is now used for services.

Next to the cathedral is the **Church of the Deposition of the Virgin's Robe** (Tserkov Rispolozheniya) built by

The Cathedral of the Assumption

architects from Pskov at the end of the 15th century. It has three low projecting apses and one dome.

To the northeast of Cathedral Square is the ★★ **Ivan the Great Bell Tower** (Kolokolnya Ivana Velikovo). The tower was completed in its present form with the two onion-shaped gilded domes under Tsar Boris Godunov around 1600, although it had been started at the beginning of the 16th century. It underwent considerable restoration in 1822, and again in1955. The smaller belfry, situated adjacent to the belltower, was constructed by Petrok Maly and one of the bells, the Uspensky Bell, weighs 70 tonnes. This bell, along with bells in 450 other churches and monasteries, has traditionally been rung at Easter, the main event in the Russian Orthodox calendar. In 1991, its chimes rang out over the city for the first time since 1918. The massive Tsar Bell *(see page 20)* stands at the foot of this tower.

Ivan the Great Bell Tower

Cathedral of the Archangel Michael

To the southeast of Cathedral Square stands the **Cathedral of the Archangel Michael** (Arkhangelsky Sobor), which was built by the Milanese architect Alevisio Novi between 1505–9. The main entrance to this cube-shaped building is in the west and the three apses are against the east wall. The central apse houses the sanctuary. Buttressed walls and annexes extend the building to the south. The roof consists of the traditional central dome on a drum and four smaller side domes at the corners. For the first time in Russia the architects incorporated the Renaissance scallop shell feature above the windows and under the *kokoshnik* gable arches.

The interior is decorated with frescoes which date from the early 16th century and were restored between 1952–66. The iconostasis dates from 1680 and **the icon of the Archangel Michael**, after whom the cathedral is named, is believed to have been the work of the most famous creator of icons, Andrei Rublev. It depicts 18 scenes from the legend of the Archangel Michael and dates from the turn of the century. The later wall decorations, painted by Simon Ushakov in the 17th century, have been restored.

Archangel Michael

All of Moscow's Grand Princes and the tsars up to Fyodor Alekseevich, who died in 1682, are buried here. Boris Godunov, however, is buried in Sergiev Posad. It also houses the tomb of Peter II, who died in 1730. Of the 46 tombstones in the cathedral vaults, the finest are those of Ivan the Terrible and of the son he murdered (according to legend), in the right side chapel behind the iconostasis, and also the reliquary of Tsarevich Dmitry by the right forward pillar.

In 1964, when the cathedral was undergoing renovation work, the tomb of Ivan the Terrible was opened. The anthropologist and sculptor Gerassimov used the bones and skull of the tsar to create a life-sized and faithful replica.

In the southwest corner of Cathedral Square stands the **Cathedral of the Annunciation** (Blagoveshchensky Sobor). This cathedral, the smallest of the three churches

around the square, is regarded as the gem of Russian sacred architecture. Built between 1484–9 for Ivan III, its three dome design was created by Pskov architects and modelled on the cathedral at Vladimir. Ivan the Terrible later enlarged the cathedral, adding another six domes on tall drums.

The Cathedral of the Annunciation

The floor inside is of polished jasper from the Ural mountains. The walls and domes are covered entirely by frescoes, which depict scenes from the Bible. Some careful restoration work undertaken in the 1960s revealed the original paintings and an inscription records that they were principally the work of Feofan Grek (Theophanes the Greek), Prokhor the Elder from Gorodyets and Andrei Rublev. Most of the iconostasis, which closes off the choir, has been attributed to Theophanes the Greek, but Rublev is credited with the icon of the Archangel Michael. Other icons can be seen in the side aisles.

The huge structure to the west of the Cathedral of the Annunciation is the **Great Kremlin Palace** (Bolshoi Kremlyovsky Dvorets). Before the dissolution of the USSR in 1991, the Great Kremlin Palace housed the assembly hall of the Supreme Soviet of the USSR and, subsequently, the Russian Parliament.

Icon detail

The Palace was built for Nicolas I by Konstantin Thon, Gerasimov and Chichagov between 1838–49, on the site of the former palace and a church, parts of which have been incorporated into the new building. The strictly proportioned main facade is 120m (410ft long) and overlooks the River Moskva to the south. An ornate staircase leads to the state rooms and the apartment used by the tsar whenever he visited Moscow. The Palace contains no fewer than 700 rooms in all.

Detail from the Great Kremlin Palace

The Great Kremlin Palace Alexandrovsky Hall

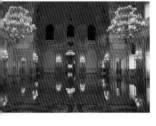

The Terem Palace

In 1934 under the supervision of architect Ivanov-Schitz, a number of rooms were combined to create the assembly hall with seating for 3,000 delegates. This is the hall which is familiar to viewers of television news reports. During the Soviet era, a huge marble statue of Lenin adorned the wall behind the podium.

The Great Kremlin Palace underwent restoration between 1992–99 and will soon be open to visitors again. A short description of the main rooms is given here.

St George's Hall is without doubt the finest room in the palace and is used for state receptions and other official ceremonies. The hall is richly ornamented with stucco mouldings and 18 convoluted zinc columns, each supporting a statue of Victory. Placed in the niches along the walls are marble slabs engraved in gold with the names of those awarded the coveted Order of St George.

St Andrew's Hall, which was once the Throne Room, and Alexander's Hall were combined to create the assembly hall of the Supreme Soviet of the USSR and the RSFSR. The Vladimir Hall, St Catherine's Hall, the Chevalier Guards Hall (a long, narrow foyer) and the Golden Room contain moiré and velvet tapestries. Those fortunate enough to gain access to these halls should look closely at the ceiling paintings and gilded vaulting. The palace contains a number of chapels and is connected to another smaller palace, which is only ever shown to visiting heads of state.

The **Church of the Nativity of the Virgin** (Tserkov Rozhdestva Bogomatery) was built in 1393 and is the oldest surviving church inside the Kremlin. Once used as the private chapel by the tsarinas, it contains 17th-century icons and frescoes from the 18th and 19th centuries. It was here on 23 September 1862 amid scenes of great splendour that the marriage of Leo Tolstoy to Sophia Behrs, a doctor's daughter, took place.

The **Terem Palace** (Teremnoy Dvorets), which stands to the north of the Great Kremlin Palace, was used by Russian rulers as a private residence. The name derives from the women's chambers in the old 15th-century palace. This five-storey baroque palace consists of many interconnected rooms some of which are linked by secret staircases. Doors are concealed in the wood panelling and others hidden by paintings. Coats of arms, plant and animal designs, some painted and some carved, are common themes throughout the interior.

One of the tsars' private rooms on the fourth floor was used as a secret meeting place and very few members of the tsars' entourage were aware of its existence. Here in 1660, the Patriarch Nikon was denounced for agreeing to a reform which threatened to split the church and the Russian empire.

The **Upper Cathedral of the Saviour** (Vercho Spassky Sobor) was built in 1635 and one of the main features is an iconostasis separating the cathedral from the Vladimir Room with a facing and royal door of beaten silver.

This church is opposite the **Golden Chamber of the Tsarina** (16th-century), one of the palace's best preserved rooms. The vaulted ceiling is supported by a single massive arch. Many 16th-century frescoes have been uncovered since restoration work started in 1947.

The **Church of the Crucifixion** (Tserkov Raspiatiya) houses a splendid iconostasis. Only the exposed parts of the body, ie face and hands, are painted, the clothes are embroidered in silk, specially commissioned in the 17th century.

A gallery connects the fourth floor of the Terem Palace with the Church of the Resurrection and St Catherine's Church, both of which were built at the beginning of the 17th century.

The **Palace of Facets** (Granovitaya Palata) used to be closed to the public, but is now open to visitors. This square palace is named after the diamond-shaped limestone blocks which pattern the main front – and is reminiscent of the Palazzo Diamanti in Ferrara. The Italian architects, Marco Ruffo and Pietro Solari, worked on the palace between 1487–91.

The ceiling of the Great Hall on the first floor is supported by four low groined vaults borne on a single pier. This vast hall (500sq m/5,400sq ft) once served as the throne room and reception room. The frescoes, which were painted in 1668 by Simeon Ushakov and renovated in the 19th century, are regarded as the finest in Russia.

25

The ★★★ **State Armoury** (Oruzheinaya Palata; open Friday–Wednesday 10am–6pm, tours at 10am, noon, 2.30pm and 4.30pm) is the richest museum in Russia, if not the whole world, with exhibits dating back to the days of Ivan the Terrible. It began as a display of arms and armour, but treasures now include spoils of war, crown jewels and insignia of the tsars and objets d'art made from enamel, ivory, silver, gold, jewellery, many of which were presented to the tsar by visiting dignitaries. The Cap of Monomakh which was used as a crown in the coronation of all the grand princes of Moscow before Peter the Great, the Hoard of Ryazan and the coronation robe of Catherine the Great are the museum's most prized possessions, but there are many other items of interest.

State Armoury exhibits

Ground floor
Exhibits include the 16th-century throne of Ivan the Terrible made from plates of ivory, Boris Godunov's 16th-

century throne, which is covered with gold-leaf, the diamond throne of Aleksei Mikhailovich and the 1682 triple throne of Ivan V, Peter I (Peter the Great) and the Regent Sofya Alekseevna.

Diamond throne

The most famous exhibit is the Cap Of Monomakh which has been wrongly linked with Vladimir Monomakh (Vladimir II d 1125). Used as the crown at the coronations of all tsars before Peter the Great, it dates from the 13th century and almost certainly originates from the Far East. Other royal insignia on display are the 16th-century crowns from the kingdom of Kazan, the crowns used by the first Romanovs and the west European-style crowns used after Peter the Great: the crowns of Catherine I and Anna Ivanovna. The ground floor rooms also contain Romanov sceptres and orbs, the robes of Peter the Great, clothes worn at the royal court, diadems, Russian and other jewellery as well as carpets made in St Petersburg.

Another ground floor room houses the collection of state coaches. The oldest coach was presented to Boris Godunov by Queen Elizabeth I of England. Other exhibits include a small coach which was made for Peter I when he was a boy, a baroque coach with door panels designed by Boucher, a large sleigh dating from 1742, Catherine the Great's coach, another coach presented by Kaiser William II and saddles, bridles and other horse trappings.

26

One of the royal coaches

First floor

Arms and armour include the 13th-century helmet of Grand Prince Yaroslav with magnificent gold and silver table-settings, sacred objects, the wedding crowns worn by Pushkin and his wife, Easter eggs made from precious metals and a Sèvres service which was presented to Alexander I by Napoleon I. Other first floor rooms house gifts presented to the Soviet Union.

The **Alexander Garden** (Aleksandrovsky Sad) runs alongside the western Kremlin wall. On the edge of Red Square, at the northern end of the garden, is the **Tomb of the Unknown Soldier**. This memorial, a low structure of red granite and black marble, commemorates all the nameless dead from the Great Fatherland War (1941–5). An eternal flame is surrounded by urns of red porphyry containing soil from the cities of Kiev, Brest, Novorossiisk, Sevastopol, Tula, Volgograd, St Petersburg (1924–91 Leningrad), Minsk and Odessa. Volgograd was 'renamed' Stalingrad on the memorial in 2004, a reference to its Soviet era name. These cities were awarded 'hero city' status at the end of the war.

Tomb of the Unknown Soldier

Since the memorial was unveiled in 1967, it has become the custom for newly-married couples to lay a bouquet of flowers on the tomb after their wedding ceremony.

Route 2

★★★ Red Square and ★★ Kitay-Gorod

Known in Russian as Krasnaya Ploschad since the October Revolution of 1917, Red Square has a double meaning: the Old Slavonic word *krasny* which normally means red, also means beautiful, as red was regarded as a particularly beautiful colour.

★★★ **Red Square** covers an area of 75,000sq m (90,000sq yds) and since the days of Ivan III in the 15th century has been the scene of many of the country's main events, including rallies, processions, demonstrations and annual markets. It was from here that the Tartars stormed the Kremlin; it is the place where patriarchs and tsars paraded in front of their people on ceremonial occasions; Kutuzov's army left from here for Borodino in 1812, and in the autumn of 1941, the defenders of Moscow took the oath of allegiance before marching to the front to face the advancing Germans. In the Soviet era, Red Square was the venue for the country's main military parade on 7 November and also for the May Day celebrations, which became a national festival.

'Beautiful' Red Square

In the northwest, Red Square is bordered by the Historical Museum, in the northeast by the GUM department store, in the southwest by the Lenin Mausoleum and in the southeast by St Basil's Cathedral. The west side of the

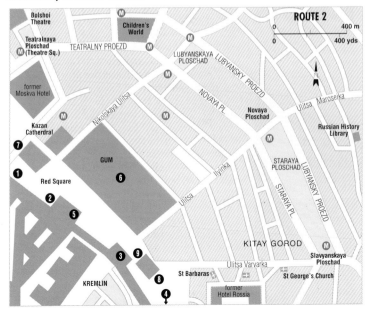

St Nicholas's Tower

Moscow's answer to Big Ben

Guards outside the Lenin Mausoleum

square with its turreted Kremlin wall and seven towers is one of the finest sights in Moscow.

To the north of the square and at the northernmost tip of the Kremlin wall stands the **Corner Arsenal** (Sobakin) **Tower** , which was built by the Italian architect Pietro Solario back in 1492. Inside the tower with its 4-m (12-ft) thick walls is a well. An underground passage used to lead from the tower to the Neglinnaya and beyond, into the city.

The **St Nicholas's Tower** ❷ (Nikolskaya Bashnya) is also the work of Solario in 1492 and is 70m (230ft) high. Named after a mosaic of the saint which can be seen above the entrance, it was destroyed by Napoleon in 1812, but rebuilt by Alexander I in the style of St Mary's Church in Stargard, Pommerania (now in Poland).

In the middle of the Kremlin's east wall stands the **Saviour's Tower** ❸ (Spasskaya Bashnya), the principal entrance to the Kremlin, although not for tourists. In the years before the revolution an icon stood above the gateway and everyone who passed through the entrance whether Russian, foreigner, serf or tsar, was required to raise their hat. The lower part of the tower was built by Solario in 1492 and the upper half, a Gothic tower, was added in 1625. The famous Kremlin carillon occupies three storeys of the tower, which reaches a height of 71m (230ft) including the red star. The clock on the Saviour's Tower is the Russian equivalent of Big Ben, with each of the four clock faces measuring 6.12m (20ft).

On the southeastern corner of the Kremlin stands the **Beklemishev Tower** ❹. This tower, which was restored to its original shape in 1949, is 46.2m (155ft) high. A canal linking the Moskva and the Neglinnaya used to run alongside the Kremlin wall, but it was drained and filled in many years ago. A grassy slope now borders the western side of Red Square and heroes of the revolution and other Soviet luminaries are buried here: Jakov Sverdlov, Felix Dzerzhinsky, Mikhail Frunze, Mikhail Kalinin, Andrei Zhdanov, Josef Vissarionovich Djugashvili (Stalin), Leonid Brezhnev, Yuri Andropov, Konstantin Chernenko. In the wall itself are urns containing the remains of Nadezhda Krupskaya (Lenin's wife), Sergei Kirov, Valerian Kuybyshev, Grigory Ordzhonikidze, Maxim Gorky, Clara Zetkin, Sen Katayama, John Reed, Fritz Heckert, Yuri Gagarin, Alexei Kosygin and others.

Set against the Kremlin wall and at the midpoint of Red Square stands the ★ **Lenin Mausoleum** ❺ (open 10am–1pm; closed Monday and Friday). After Lenin's death in January 1924, his body was first placed in a wooden mausoleum, which served not only as the Soviet hero's resting place, but also as a reviewing platform for members of the Government at military and civil parades. In 1930, however, Shchusev built the present structure in dark red granite. The guards who once stood outside the mausoleum were disbanded by Boris Yeltsin at the end of 1993. With the queues of people wishing to pay their respects to the founder of the Soviet state getting ever shorter, there is considerable debate about what should be done with Lenin's body. Many feel that it should be given the proper burial that Lenin himself requested.

Opposite the Kremlin on the east side of Red Square is the biggest department store in Russia, the **GUM** ❻ (Gosudarstvenny Universalny Magazin). Built in 1890, this three-storey building 90m (300ft) wide and 250m (825ft) long was designed by Pomerantshev in Russian style and it employs 4,000 sales assistants. Now privatised, it consists of several expensive boutiques and small shops.

Between the GUM department store and the Historical Museum stands the **Kazan Cathedral**, rebuilt and newly consecrated on its original site. On the north side of Red Square is the ★ **Historical Museum** ❼ (Istorichesky Muzey; Monday, Wednesday–Saturday 10am–6pm, Sunday 11am–8pm, last tickets 1 hour before closing; closed the first Saturday of the month). This red brick building was built at the end of the 19th century by the English and Russian architects Sherwood and Semyonov on the site of 18th-century Moscow University. The Historical Museum became the main museum of the Soviet Union, documenting the history of the Soviet people from pre-historic times. It is presently under renovation and is due to acquire further exhibits taken from the old Lenin Museum. In front of the museum is a statue of the Soviet hero, Marshal Zhukov.

To the south of Red Square, stands the extraordinary ★★ **St Basil's Cathedral** ❽ (Sobor Vasiliya Blazhen-

The Historical Museum

GUM – rich pickings

novo). This amazing structure was built by Ivan the Terrible in the middle of the 16th century to celebrate his victory over Tartars in Kazan – a victory which opened the way to the Urals and beyond.

St Basil's Cathedral

According to the legend, Ivan was so struck by the beauty of St Basil's that he had the architect, Posnik Yakovlev, blinded, so that he would not be able to build anything more beautiful for another ruler.

The ground plan of the cathedral forms a cross with four chapels at the end of each arm. The principal chapel lies at the centre, with four smaller chapels between this and the larger chapels, making a total of nine chapels in all. The array of onion-shaped domes, smaller towers and tent-like *kokoshnik* gables are not so confusing as they first appear as they were planned on strict geometric principles.

The first chapel by the entrance contains an exhibition of 16th-century Russian architecture. The huge lower storey serves as a support for the nine domes. One room displays a collection of 16th-century Russian and Tartar fire-arms. A steep, narrow staircase inside one of the walls leads into the principal chapel and an inner gallery links all the tower chapels. The eight chapels were dedicated to the saints for the days on which the battle of Kazan had taken place. The ninth chapel was built in 1588 as a resting place for the wandering monk, Basil the Blessed.

The interior is less impressive than the grandiose towers. In 1954, some notable frescoes and sculptures were uncovered, which probably date from the cathedral's construction. In two rooms under the belltower, old prints and plans are exhibited.

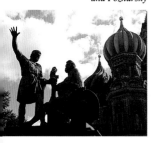

Monument to Minin and Pozharsky

In front of St Basil's stands the **Monument to Minin and Pozharsky ❾**, Moscow's first patriotic monument, dedicated to two popular heroes who saved the city from an invasion of Polish and Lithuanian troops at the beginning of the 17th century. The followers of citizen Minin and Prince Pozharsky combined to oust the invaders first from Kitay-Gorod and then from the Kremlin, recapturing Moscow in 1612. Lomonosov invited the public to subscribe to the costs of the monument and in 1818, Ivan Martos' monument was unveiled.

Opposite Ulitsa Ilyinka is a small stone mound, called the Lobnoye Mesto or Place of Execution. The tsar's decrees were proclaimed here and it is believed that a wooden platform nearby was used to carry out public executions.

We now enter the ★★★ **Kitay-Gorod District**, centred on three streets, Ulitsa Varvarka, Ulitsa Ilinka and Nikolskaya Ulitsa.

The word *gorod* means town and *kitay* comes from an old Tartar word meaning sandbag. Sandbags for use in case of fire have been found in the town's fortifications. Kitay-Gorod now refers to the district of Moscow to the east of the Kremlin, where, since the 15th century, merchants, artisans, hawkers and popular entertainers from Russia and beyond have lived. The powerful occupants of the nearby Kremlin needed their products and their skills and a mutually beneficial relationship developed between the two quarters.

In the 16th century, a red stone wall with narrow defensive windows was built around the quarter and a few fragments of the fortress wall can still be seen in Nikolskaya Ulitsa and in Teatralnaya Ploschad. For centuries, Kitay-Gorod has retained its inner courtyards, its winding alleys and the individuality of its inhabitants and a look inside just one of the existing courtyards is sufficient to gain an impression of Moscow's past.

Monk and nun collecting money in Nikolskaya Ulitsa

Nikolskaya Ulitsa is probably the best place to start a tour of this area. It begins opposite the St Nicholas Tower on the Kremlin wall and runs parallel to Ulitsa Ilyinka. One of the first houses on the left, dating from 1740, was used as a debtors' prison and in the rear courtyard stands the even older Mint House (Monetny Dvor). In 1775, the peasant leader Pugachov and some of his followers were held here before their execution.

Further to the left, in the courtyard of No. 7, lie some of remains of the Zaikonospassky monastery which was built around 1600 and then rebuilt in 1680 by Ivan Zarudny on the orders of Peter the Great. In 1687, the monastery was converted into the Slav-Greek-Latin Academy, Russia's first establishment for higher education.

The Zaikonospassky Monastery

On the left, a preservation order protects the building at No. 15 with its delightful green-white facade. Built by Bakarev and Mironovsky in 1814, it combines Gothic

No. 15, Nikolskaya Ulitsa

elements and the old Russian architectural style. On the right, in the side street to the right, stand the remains of the Bogoyavlensky Monastery's church, built in Moscow Baroque in 1696.

At 21 Nikolskaya Ulitsa is one of Moscow's first chemists, once known as the Ferrein Drugstore after its German owner. This splendid shop was built in 1896 by Erichsohn. Nearby is one of Moscow's most exclusive shopping streets, **Tretyakov Passage**. It is packed with luxury cars, stylish women and super-rich oligarchs buying baubles at Gucci, Tiffany and other exclusive boutiques.

Ulitsa Ilyinka runs parallel to Nikolskaya Ulitsa on the southeast side of the GUM department store. On the right an entire block is occupied by the former **Merchant Arcade** (Stary Gostiny Dvor), built between 1791–1805 by Quarenghi. A little further is the old Mercantile Exchange (Birzha), now the headquarters of the Russian Chamber of Commerce.

The Chamber of Commerce

From the southern end of Red Square runs ★★**Ulitsa Varvarka**, which is now something of an open-air museum. On the right side of the street is the Church of St Barbara (Tserkov-Varvary) – one of the finest examples of Russian Classical architecture. It stands alongside the 17th-century Maxim Church. Situated behind these two churches is a building which was presented to Ivan the Terrible in 1556 by English merchants and during the 15th and 16th centuries, it was the residence of the English ambassador. It has been restored and now houses an exhibition of archaeological finds from the Moscow area.

The most interesting buildings in this street are the Znamensky (Omen) Monastery with its five domes and, next door (No. 10), the ancestral home of the Romanov family, a boyar town house dating from the 17th century. It has now been carefully restored and houses a branch of the Historical Museum, which documents the traditions of the boyar families. A little further on looms the construction site of the former Rossia Hotel complex. Right at the end of Varvarka Street stands the small 17th-century Church of St George with five domes and in a nearby side street, Nikitnov Pereulok, is the ★**Church of the Trinity in Nikitniki**. Here Simon Ushakov's frescoes in the upper storey add to the richly ornamented interior.

Church of the Trinity in Nikitniki

The remains of the Kitay-Gorod brick walls can be seen on the right at the end of Varvarka Street before it merges with Slavianskaya Ploschad at the monument to Cyrill and Mephodiy, two Slavic saints who designed the Russian (Cyrillic) alphabet. Only the Church of All Saints has survived. It was built by Prince Dmitry Donskoy in the 16th century in memory of the Russian soldiers who fell in battle. Renovation work in the 17th and 18th centuries changed the facade considerably.

Ploschad Varvarka and Ulitsa Solyanka, which runs into the square from the southeast, are strictly speaking not part of the Kitay-Gorod quarter, but belong to the White City *(see page 12)*. Nevertheless, the atmosphere and architectural features of the two quarters have much in common as they both date from the 16th century. The name of the street derives from the salt stores (solyany sklady) which were to be found here in the 17th and 18th centuries. Some yellowy-white merchant houses from this period have been well preserved. On the left-hand side of the street (No. 5) stands the Church of the Nativity of the Most Holy Virgin, built in 1764. On the right-hand side (No. 14) is the former Guardianship Council, the institution in charge of financing the Foundling (children's) Home at No. 12. Designed by Blank in the Empire style by Giliardi and Grigorev in 1825, it now houses the Russian Academy of Medical Science.

The Church of the Trinity in Serebrianiki

Further on stands the tall belltower of the 18th-century Church of the Trinity in Serebrianiki, which is another Blank creation.

To the left of Ulitsa Solyanka and bordered to the north by Ulitsa Bogdana-Khmelnitskovo is a network of narrow alleys covering the site of the tsar's 16th-century apple orchards. They contain some well preserved old buildings, such as the Church of St Vladimir, which stands at the end of Starosadsky Pereulok, built by Alevisio Novi in 1510. Alongside is the old St John Convent surrounded by huge fortified walls and towers.

Other interesting buildings include the 17th-century house of the boyar Shusky in Podkopayevsky Pereulok and the 16th-century house of Hetmans Mazeppa at 10 Kolpachny Pereulok.

Hetmans Mazeppa's house

Ulitsa Maroseika, which is a continuation of Ulitsa Ilyinka to the east of Novaya Ploschad, is another interesting street. The oldest building here is the tiny red and white Church of St Nicholas the Wonder-Worker, which dates from 1657. No. 11 is the house which was built for the boyar Naryshkin in the 17th century and which later became a girls' school run by the German Pastor Glück. During the Great Northern War (1700–21) which Russia waged against Sweden, the pastor was living in Marienburg (modern Aluksne, Latvia), on land occupied by the Russian army of Peter the Great. A maid in the pastor's house was Martha Skavronsky, the daughter of a Lithuanian peasant. The Russian tsar fell in love with her, so in 1712 she became his second wife. In 1724 she was crowned tsarina and on his death became Catherine I, and ruled Russia for the next two years.

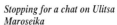

Stopping for a chat on Ulitsa Maroseika

The most interesting sight in this street, however, is the Church of Saints Kosmas and Damian, a splendid example of Russian Classicism.

Route 3

Okhotny Ryad and nearby squares

The Turkish War Memorial

Slavianskaya Ploschad, Staraya Ploschad, Novaya Ploschad, Lubyanskaya Ploschad (fromerly Ploschad Dzerzhinskovo) and Okhotny Ryad all lie on the inner ring road, which skirts around the east, north and west of the city centre.

To the north of Ploschad Varvarka is **Staraya Ploschad** (Old Square), where a chapel has been erected to the memory of the Russian grenadiers who died at Plevna in the Russo-Turkish War of 1877–8. On the south side of Staraya Ploschad was the headquarters of the Communist Party of the USSR, which was banned by Boris Yeltsin.

To the north of Old Square is **Novaya Ploschad** (New Square). The imposing building to the northeast of the square is the ★ **Polytechnic Museum ⑩** (Politeknichesky Muzey; Tuesday–Sunday 10am–6.30pm, closed the last Thursday in the month). It was built between 1877–96 by Monighetti and Chochin. More than 50 rooms contain well over 20,000 exhibits which attempt to explain the technological advances made in such fields as mining, chemicals, electronics, space travel, telecommunications and vehicle construction.

Polytechnic Museum plaque

34

Directly opposite on the southwest side of Novaya Ploschad (No. 12), stands the 19th-century Church of St John the Divine, which now houses the **Museum of the History of Moscow City ⑪** (Muzey Istorii Goroda Moskvy; Sunday, Tuesday, Thursday and Saturday 10am–6pm,

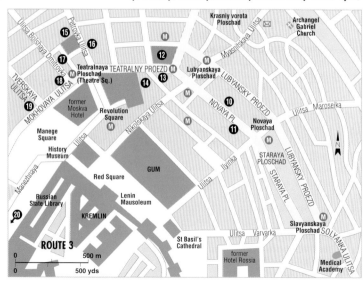

Wednesday and Friday 11am–7pm, last tickets 1 hour before closing; closed Monday and the last day of the month). On display is a large collection of town plans, models, pictures and photographs documenting the changes which have taken place in the city, particularly since its destruction in 1812, those made after the Revolution and again after World War II.

Teatralny Proezd

35

At the north end of the square is **Lubyanskaya Ploschad** (Lubyanka Square). Formerly known as Ploschad Dzerzhinskovo after one of Lenin's closest associates and a founder of the KGB, a monument to the Soviet hero stood in the middle of the square. But in August 1991 after the failed coup against Gorbachev, the crowds cheered as the cranes hauled down his statue. But the north side of the square is still dominated by the KGB headquarters building, the notorious Lubyanka.

Entrance to the former KGB headquarters

On the left is the entrance to Lubyanka Metro station, formerly Dzerzhinskaya, and to the northwest, one of Russia's biggest children's toy shops, **Detsky Mir ⑫** or Children's World. Constructed in 1957 on the site of the Moscow foundry where the Tsar Cannon was cast, it is a children's paradise.

Taking in the sights

Teatralny Proezd leads off to the west, but on the south side of the street, in a small garden, stands a monument by Volnukhin to Russia's printing pioneer, Ivan Fedorov ⑬. The statue dates from 1909, but Fedorov is said to have printed the first Russian book for the church in 1563. Ivan the Terrible set up the first church printing house, which was split up later into a number of smaller private printing houses. It was in the **Printers' Court** (Pechatny Dvor), now the History and Archives Institute, where the Orthodox Synod's printing house produced the first Russian language version of the Acts of the Apostles. The book is now on display in the Historical Museum.

Once a good place for book collectors to browse, the Knizhnaya Nachodka antique book store that stood behind Federov's monument is no longer there. Nearby are the remains of Kitay-Gorod's old wall *(see page 31)* with a gateway into Nikolskaya Ulitsa.

The **Hotel Metropol** ⓮ (Gostinitsa Metropol) is situated a short distance to the west. It was one of the few top-class hotels built before World War I (1899–1903). Fully restored in 1990, it contains a large antique bookshop and Intourist's central booking office for boat, rail and air travel.

The Hotel Metropol

We now come to ★ **Teatralnaya Ploschad**. In the middle of the square is a granite bust of the philosopher Karl Marx. The foundation stone for this monument was laid by Lenin in 1920 and the plinth is inscribed with some of Marx's most famous words: 'Workers of the world unite'. But amid the celebrations of August 1991, a bronze inscription was attached to the monument: Workers of the world forgive me.

This square with its extensive lawns and gardens, spring flowers and fountains is one of the prettiest parts of central Moscow. One of the world's most famous theatres flanks its north side, the ★★ **Bolshoi Theatre** ⓯ (Bolshoy Teatr). The Bolshoi or Grand Theatre was built in 1824 following designs by Beauvais and Mikhailov. Cavos rebuilt it in 1856 after it was burnt down and it has remained largely unchanged.

The Bolshoi Theatre

The impressive structure is a masterpiece of Classical design with eight huge columns bearing a sculptured tympanum topped by a bronze quadriga. The stage is 26m (80ft) wide, 23m (75ft) deep and 18m (60ft) high. The auditorium with five tiers has seating for more than 2,000. The white and gold interior complements the dark red upholstery. The opera and ballet company includes over 100 soloists, a choir of 200 singers, an orchestra with 250 musicians and 250 ballet dancers.

For over a century, the Bolshoi has been synonymous with the very best in the world of music and theatre. Richard Wagner conducted a concert here in 1863 and is said to have always had fond memories of his visit, because of the huge fee he received.

Bolshoi ballerina

The history of the theatre is closely linked with the events of 1917. A bitter struggle took place between the Red Guard who had sought shelter there and the White Army cadets who were encamped in the Metropol Hotel. Important political meetings also took place in the Bolshoi, the most notable being Lenin's declaration in 1922 of the foundation of the Federation of Soviet Socialist Republics, the forerunner to the Soviet Union.

Unfortunately, natural forces have also taken their toll on the structure. The underground Neglinnaya River and the rumblings of the city's metro system have caused serious subsidence problems to the structure and restoration works have forced it to close for the near future.

Alexander Ostrovsky

Just to the east of the Bolshoi Theatre is the **Maly Theatre ⓰** (Little Teatr). This theatre was built to honour the dramatist Mikhail Shchepkin and was also known as Shchepkin House. Another neoclassical building, it was constructed in 1821, but with a smaller stage which was better suited to one-man performances, plays and comedies. A bust of the Russian dramatist, Alexander Ostrovsky, is a reminder of the close links which existed between him and this theatre, where nearly all of his works were performed. Maxim Gorky described this theatre as the 'university of the Russian peoples'.

Opposite the Little Theatre on the west side of Teatralnaya Ploschad is a third theatre, the **Children's Theatre ⓱** (Detsky Teatr). Opened as a children's theatre on Lenin's initiative in 1921, its repertoire consists mainly of plays for young people, and the majority of the actors are young.

The Children's Theatre

On the corner of Ulitsa Bolshaya Dmitrovka is the **House of Unions ⓲** (Dom Soyuzov) which, prior to the Revolution, was the Nobles' Club. Originally, the mansion belonged to Prince Vasily Dolgoruky-Krimsky and boasted the smartest ballroom in Moscow. The white and gold Hall of Columns (Kolonny Zal) is now used as a concert venue. Klara Schumann, Franz Liszt, Tchaikovsky, Rimsky-Korsakov and Rachmaninov all played here. Pushkin, Lermontov and Tolstoy were frequent guests at the balls and civic ceremonies and in their books they all describe the splendid hall with its white marble columns. Lenin often spoke here and when he died in 1924, his body lay in state in the Hall of Columns so that the people of Moscow could pay their respects.

The Hotel Moskva

Across Okhotny Ryad lies **Revolutsii Ploschad** (Revolution Square), the scene of many bloody street battles in October 1917. On the southeast edge of the square stands a red brick building, Moscow's old administrative headquarters, dating from 1890. More recently it housed the Central Lenin Museum, which was closed in November 1993. Some exhibits have been transferred to the Historical Museum *(see page 29)*, although not all are on display.

On Okhotny Ryad, is the building which houses the state Duma (Gosydarstvenaya Duma), the lower chamber of the Russian Parliament. It was once the office of the state planning committee (Gosplan). Beyond the junction with Tverskaya Ulitsa is the site of the former 22-storey Intourist Hotel. The hotel was demolished in 2004 and a new modern hotel complex is due to replace it. On the corner of Tverskaya Ulitsa is the **National Hotel ⓳** (Gostinitsa Nasional), built prior to World War I as a luxury hotel but which is currently closed, awaiting development.

Okhotny Ryad is bordered to the south by the vast **Manezhnaya Ploschad** (Manege Square), which is now a shopping and leisure complex, and a meeting place for young Muscovites. Completed in time for the 850th anniversary of Moscow, it consists of an underground mall, car park, and excavations museum (exhibiting items unearthed during construction work); and an upper level with a pedestrian area surrounded by restaurants and cafés. Created by the prolific and controversial architect Zurad Tseretely, the design represents a river, with fountains, old fashioned lanterns and statues of fairytale characters.

Moscow State University

The yellow and white building on the right hand side of the square is the Journalism Faculty of the Moscow State University, named after Lomonosov (Moscovsky Gosudarstveny Universitet imeni Lomonosova, or MGU). It was built in the late 18th century by Matvey Kazakov, and restored in 1917–19. The imposing neoclassical building next to it is the university's Institute of Asia and Africa, behind which is the Faculty of Psychology. The other 12 faculties of MGU, as well as student accommodation, are now located on a new site out in the Vorobiov Hills *(see page 54)*.

38

State Library plaque

On the left are the remains of the former Riding School for Officers (Manege). This historical building, designed in 1817 by the French military engineer, Montferrand, burnt down in mysterious circumstances in 2004.

A long block on the right-hand side of Mokhovaya Ulitsa is the **Russian State Library** (Rossiyskaya Gosudarstvennaya Biblioteka). This huge library, the biggest in Russia and possibly the world, which used to be known as the Lenin Library, can accommodate 2,500 visitors in its 25 reading rooms. Adjacent to the building is a nine-storey repository containing close to 36 million books. In front of the entrance there is a new statue of the famous writer Fiodor Dostoevsky.

Just behind the newer State Library is the **Pashkov Mansion ㉒** (Dom Pashkov), designed by one of Russia's most famous architects, Vasily Bazhenov. It was built between 1784–6 in Classical style and, like others from this era, it is a wooden construction with a plaster finish. Originally housing the Rumiantsev Museum, where paintings and manuscripts were exhibited, it was later converted into a public library. In 1940, the architects Helfreich and Shchuko created the portico out of dark marble.

The main facade displays sculptures of famous poets, while on the side facing Ulitsa Vozdvizhonka are portraits of famous academics. Underneath the library complex is the *Biblioteka imeni Lenina Metro station*.

Route 4

Between Bolshaya Nikitskay and Myasnitskaya ulitsas

The following section describes that part of the city to the north of Okhotny Ryad and between the roads which radiate northwards from the Kremlin. The Boulevard Ring (Bulvarnoye Koltso), which partially encircles the Kremlin in a wide horseshoe shape, bisects the district.

The route begins in **Bolshaya Nikitskay Ulitsa** at No. 13, the **Tchaikovsky Conservatory** ㉑ (Gosudarstvennaya Konservatoriya imeni Pyetra Tchaiykovskovo). This splendid, acoustically perfect concert hall with seating for 1800 is the venue for the International Tchaikovsky Competition. The small concert hall with 444 seats is reserved for chamber music. The conservatory was founded in 1866 by Anton Rubinstein and both Rachmaninov and David Oistrakh studied and taught here. In front of the yellow and white horseshoe-shaped building stands a Tchaikovsky memorial by Vera Mukhina (1946).

Bolshaya Nikitskaya Ulitsa

At No. 19 Bolshaya Nikitskay Ulitsa is the superbly equipped **Mayakovsky Theatre** ㉒ (Mayakovsky Teatr), which includes contemporary, avant-garde and classical productions in its repertoire. Founded in 1922 by the poet Meyerhold, it adopted his name when he died in 1930.

Tchaikovsky memorial

39

At the junction of Bolshaya Nikitskay Ulitsa and Nikitsky Bulvar are the premises of TASS, the state press agency, and in the middle of the boulevard stands a statue of Timiryazev (1923), a celebrated agronomist and botanist.

At No. 7 Leontevsky Pereulok, which forks off to the right directly in front of the TASS offices, is the ★★**Mu-**

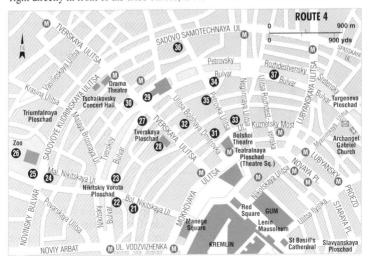

ROUTE 4

Moscow Zoo

1950 skyscraper block

Yeliseevsky food shop

seum of **Russian Folk Art** ㉓ (Tuesday and Thursday noon– 7.30pm, closed Monday, otherwise daily 11am– 5.30pm), with a wide sample of Russian handicrafts.

The actor and producer Konstantin Stanislavsky lived in the house opposite (No. 6) from 1921 until his death in 1938 and a small museum commemorates the life of the founder of Moscow's Art Theatre.

Bolshaya Nikitskay Ulitsa crosses the Garden (Sadovoye) Ring and ends in **Ploschad Kudrinskaya** ㉔. This square was previously known as Ploschad Vosstaniya (Uprising Square) after the the struggles that took place between 1905–17, when workers in this quarter took to the streets and set up barricades. It has now reverted to its original name, which refers to the nearby village. On the west side of the square is a skyscraper block built in 1950 with 452 apartments. At ground level is a food shop and a cinema. The wings have 18 storeys and the main tower 24 storeys, which reach a height of 160m (500ft).

On the north side of the square is a fine, Classical building with a triangular tympanum supported by eight pillars. Known as the **Widows' House** ㉕, it was built by the Italian Giliardi between 1809–11 and in the 19th century housed the widows and orphans of soldiers and civil servants. It is now a further education centre for doctors.

The short Barrikadnaya Ulitsa (Barricade Street) then becomes Ulitsa Krasnoy Presni, which joins Ploschad Vosstaniya from the west. On the right-hand side of Ulitsa Krasnoy Presni is **Moscow Zoo** ㉖ (Zoopark; winter 10am–5pm; summer 10am–8pm; closed Monday). Nearest Metro station: Krasnopresnenskaya. The entrance is at No. 1 Bolshaya Gruzinskaya Ulitsa. Founded in 1864 by Bogdanov, an academic, it contains over 3,000 mammals, birds, reptiles and fish, which are kept as far as possible in their natural habitats. The zoo's veterinary research institute investigates animal feeds, the causes of animal diseases, and how animals adjust to domestication.

Primarily a shopping and commercial thoroughfare, the **Tverskaya Ulitsa** (Tver Street), is considered by its residents to be one of the city's prettiest streets. There are three sections as the road heads northwest: the first section from Okhotny Ryad to Tverskaya Ploschad, from there to Pushkinskaya Ploschad with the final section, another important area for theatres, as far as Ploschad Mayakovskovo Square on the Garden (Sadovoye) Ring. Tverskaya Ulitsa is the first stage of the old road to St Petersburg via Tver and Great Novgorod. In 1932, the street was renamed Ulitsa Gorkovo after Maxim Gorky, the Russian writer and exponent of Socialist Realism, but in 1990 its original name was restored. In 1937, this important route out of Moscow had to be widened to cope with the increasing traffic. Many of the street's older buildings had to be demolished as the width of the carriageway was more than doubled. Many new apartment blocks now line the street and apart from the Telegraph Office, the only old building which remains from the days before the road widening, is No. 5, the Yermolova Theatre, which is named after a famous Russian actress.

At the junction with Kamergersky Pereulok Teatra is the ★★**Moscow Chekhov Arts Theatre** (MXT), which was founded by the two actors and producers Stanislavsky and Nemirovich-Danchenko in 1898. Their approach to stage production influenced European theatre at the turn of the century. The picture of the seagull on the curtain is a reminder of Chekhov's most important play *The Seagull*, which was deemed a failure until revived by Stanislavsky. In 1987, the theatre company split into two groups, MCHAT-I and MCHAT-II. MCHAT-II have found a home in the **Teatr Druzhby Narodov** at 22 Tverskoy Bulvar **㉗** (The Theatre of the Friendship of the People).

Tver Street's first major junction is at **Tsverskaya Ploschad**. The equestrian statue at the centre of the square shows Yury Dolgorukiy, traditionally regarded as Moscow's founder *(see page 11)*. On the left the old residence of Moscow's Governors is now the **residence of the Mayor of Moscow ㉘**. It was built by Kazakov in 1782, and Lenin often addressed the workers from the balcony. In 1937, it was aligned with the present row of buildings and in 1946, it was enlarged and modernised. On the south side of the square stood the Hotel Dresden, where many west European and Russian celebrities stayed. After 1917, it became the headquarters of the Red Guard. Tverskaya Ulitsa continues to Pushkinskaya Ploschad.

On the right-hand side of Tverskaya Ulitsa is one of Moscow's most beautiful food halls, Yeliseevsky, with an interesting interior in Russian art nouveau style. It was owned by the rich Yeliseev family, traders who left Rus-

41

Statue of Yury Dolgorukiy and Tsverskaya Ploschad

Pushkin's statue and Square

Outside the Museum of Modern Russian History

The Tchaikovsky Concert Hall

sia after the 1917 Revolution. The writer Nikolai Ostrovsky lived in this part of Tverskaya Ulitsa and his flat has been converted into a museum.

★ **Pushkinskaya Ploschad** ❷❾ (Pushkin Square), named after Russia's most distinguished poet and writer, is the next major junction and home to the first McDonalds restaurant in the city. What was, until 1930, the Convent of the Passion of Jesus is situated by the square; it is now the centre of the Russian press. On the north side are the *Izvestia* offices and the buildings to the south house the editorial offices of many other newspapers and magazines. The middle of the square is dominated by a statue of Pushkin and on the east side is the huge cinema, the Pushkinsky, with seating for 2,500. A house behind the cinema was the home of the celebrated composer and pianist Sergei Rachmaninov. One of the roads leading off the square which runs parallel to Tverskaya Ulitsa is Ulitsa Malaya Dmitrovka. One of the first buildings in this street is a 17th-century church, the Church of the Nativity of Our Lady in Putniki (Tserkov Rozhdestva Bogoroditsy v Putinkakh), an example of early Moscow architecture.

Nearby you can find a good sushi restaurant, Yaponsky Gorodsky (Gnezdnikovsky Per 9, tel: 229 2108). Sushi is amazingly popular in Moscow – strange given that the city is one of the most landlocked capitals on earth – and sushi bars can be found all over the city.

Northwest of Tverskoy Bulvar, at No. 21 Tverskaya Ulitsa, is the ★★ **Museum of Modern Russian History** ❸⓿ (Muzey Sovremennoi Istorii Rossii; Tuesday–Saturday 10am–6pm, Sunday 10am–5pm, last tickets 1 hour before closing; closed last Friday of the month). The displays document the history of Russia before, during and after the Revolution with special emphasis on the years between 1905–17 and also World War II. It is housed in a former aristocratic fraternity house belonging to Prince Razumovsky, which was built in 1780 by Giliardi and altered by Menelas in 1818. A tram used as a barricade during the 1991 coup attempt is now parked outside. An annex of the Museum of the Revolution, the Krasnaya Presnya Museum, is situated at 4 Bolshoy Pzetechensky Pereulok, near Krasnopresnenskaya Metro station (Tuesday–Sunday 11am–6pm). A little further north on the left-hand side is the Mossoviet Theatre and then, on the Sadovoye Ring, the Tchaikovsky Concert Hall with seating for 1,500.

Ulitsa Bolshaya Dmitrovka is another important road in this district of Moscow. It runs parallel to Tverskaya Ulitsa starting at the northeast end of Okhotny Ryad opposite the Moscow Hotel.

At No. 6 is the **Operetta Theatre** ❸❶ (Teatr Operetty), where many well known 19th-century Russian operas were first performed. Fyodor Shalyapin also sang here. The busy **Stoleshnikov Pereulok** ❸❷ (Stoleshnikov Lane) crosses

Bolshaya Dmitrovka about half way along, and the section to the right has been turned into a lively pedestrian shopping zone with a wide selection of shops. There are a number of specialist retailers here, selling interesting and unusual souvenirs, including furs, gold and silver jewellery, amber, lacquer work, handicrafts and Crimean sparkling wine.

Ulitsa Petrovka is another busy thoroughfare which begins at Teatralnaya between the Bolshoi Theatre and the TSUM and runs parallel to Pushkin Street. **TSUM ㉝** (Tsentralny Universalny Magazin) is the second biggest department store in Moscow. The wide range of shops here and in Petrovka Passage has been popular with shoppers since before the Revolution. It is now semi-privatised. At No. 30 you can find Taras Bulba (Ulitsa Petrokva 30/7, tel: 284 3019), a restaurant specialising in Ukrainian food, named after the hero of Gogol's novel of the same name.

A short distance from the Boulevard Ring in Ulitsa Petrovka is a two-storey red brick building, the ★ **Peter Monastery ㉞** (Petrovsky Monastir) and the restored Church of Peter the Metropolitan (both open Wednesday to Sunday noon–6pm). This fortified monastery was built by Prince Dmitry Donskoy, but it is now used as a Literature Museum and there is a permanent exhibition on Russian literature of the 17th and 18th centuries.

Opposite is a Classical town house ㉟, built in 1790 by Kazakov for a rich merchant, but which now houses a medical institute.

The continuation of Ulitsa Petrovka beyond the Boulevard Ring is called Karyetny Ryad, or Carriage Row. The name refers to the time when, in the late 18th century, carriages were made and sold here. The building on the left-hand side at No. 1, which was built by Kazakov in 1775, is now a hospital, although it was formerly a mansion belonging to Prince Gagarin.

A little further north on the left-hand side is **Hermitage Park ㊱** (Sad Ermitazh), an open space laid out in Classical style with lakes, marble statues and shady avenues. Other amenities include a summer theatre, an open-air stage, a restaurant and several cafés.

Ulitsa Neglinnaya (Neglinnaya Street) owes its name to the river, whose course it now follows. In the days of Catherine the Great, the river was channelled underground to prevent flooding and eliminate marshy ground. Consequently the road runs at a slightly lower level than the side streets. One of these side streets, the Kuznetsky Most (Smith's Bridge) was the bridge over the Neglinnaya where the blacksmiths worked.

After the fire of Moscow in 1812, Ulitsa Neglinnaya was rebuilt in the Empire style and the unity and harmony of the architecture resembles some of the old streets of St Petersburg. One of the imposing buildings from the last

43

Trading on Kuznetsky Most

The Russian State Bank

century (No. 12) is now the headquarters of the **Russian State Bank**. No. 14, a fine building with a small courtyard in an unusual Moorish style, is a popular centre for collectors of bank notes.

Ulitsa Neglinnaya broadens out where it crosses the Boulevard Ring and the square at the junction is called Trubnaya Ploschad. It used to be the site of a busy flower, bird and dog market in pre-Revolution days. A similar market, daily 8am–2pm, is now held in Kalitnikovskaya Sredniaya Ulitsa, which is near Taganka Square on the eastern edge of the inner city. Trubnaya Square is now just a busy junction, where Ulitsa Neglinnaya becomes Tsvetnoy Bulvar. The Old Circus (No. 13) and the Central Market (No. 15) are both now situated along this attractive boulevard.

Central Market at No. 15

Ulitsa Rozhdestvenka (Rozhdestvenka Street) is another of the roads heading north from near Detsky Mir, the children's toy shop in Teatralny Proezd. It runs parallel to Ulitsa Neglinnaya. One of the first buildings is the Savoy Hotel. Three hundred years ago, the side street, Pushetshnaya Ulitsa or Cannon Street, was the site for the foundry where the Russian army's cannon were cast.

Nearby, in Kuznetsky Most, is one of Moscow's very few vegetarian restaurants. Including a take-away section and food shop, Djagannat (Ulitsa Kuznetsky Most 11, tel: 928 3580) is a real rarity in mostly meat-obsessed Moscow.

At the junction of Ulitsa Rozhdestvenka and the Boulevard Ring, or Rozhdestvensky Bulvar as this section of it is called, the remains of the brick wall and belltower of the **Nativity Convent** ❸❼ (Rozhdestvensky Monastir) can be seen. This monastery was founded in the 16th century by the mother of Prince Vladimir of Serpukhov. The main chapel in the inner courtyard was built between 1501–5 and it is one of the oldest sacred buildings in Moscow. **Bolshaya Lubyanka Ulitsa** runs from Lubyanka Square to the Boulevard Ring, becoming first Ulitsa Stretenka and then Prospekt Mira as it continues towards the northeast.

Until 1953, the headquarters of the Soviet Foreign Ministry stood on the corner of Kuznetsky Most, but it is now housed in the skyscraper in Smolensk Square. The monument in front of the old ministry building commemorates Vorovsky, a Soviet diplomat, who was assassinated in Lausanne in 1923.

Richard Wagner stayed here

The 18th-century green-painted baroque mansion just beyond the Yeliseevsky food hall features in Tolstoy's *War and Peace* and the composer Richard Wagner stayed at No. 9 on the left-hand side. A little further on, again on the left-hand side, the remains of Sretensky Monastery that goes back to 1395 can be seen. A section of the monastery's 17th-century chapel has been preserved.

Mayakovsky's room and bust

At the beginning of Sretenka Ulitsa is the small Church of the Dormition at Pechatniki, which was built in the late 17th century. Laid out in the 17th century, this street, unaffected by the fire of 1812, is at the heart of a busy commercial district but has no other points of interest.

Myasnitskaya Ulitsa (Myasnitskaya Street), formerly Ulitsa Kirova, starts at Lubyanskaya Ploschad and heads in a northeast direction towards the Leningrad main-line railway station. During the 19th century it was one of Moscow's busiest thoroughfares.

45

At the start of Myasnitskaya Ulitsa, a smaller side street, Lubyansky Proezd, forks to the right and at Nos 3–6 is the **Mayakovsky Museum** (Muzey Mayakovskovo; Monday 10am–6pm, Thursday 1–6pm, Tuesday, Friday, Saturday and Sunday noon–6pm, closed Wednesday). It is devoted to the memory of one of Russia's most important constructivist poets, who rented this space as an office, but shot himself there in 1930.

The Intourist headquarters are located on Milyutinskaya Ulitsa, off Ulitsa Myasnitskaya. Enjoying a complete monopoly during Soviet times, Intourist now faces competition from private tourist agencies, but is still the biggest player on the scene.

At No. 26 Myasnitskaya Ulitsa is Moscow's General Post Office (Moskovsky Pochtant). The building opposite at No. 21 was erected in the late 18th century by the architect Vassili Bazhenov and during the 19th century was used as a school of painting, sculpture and architecture.

The Archangel Gabriel Church

Behind the General Post Office is the ★**Archangel Gabriel Church**, which was built between 1701–7 by Ivan Zarudny for Grand Prince Menshikov. Also known as the Menshikov Tower, it is regarded as one of the finest baroque churches in Moscow and many experts believe it marks a transitional stage between old Russian style and the towered structures typical of Classical St Petersburg.

Statue of Lenin's wife,
Garden Boulevard

Turgenevskaya Ploschad is situated at the junction of Myasnitskaya Ulitsa and the Garden Boulevard. The Metro station Chistiye Prudi, formerly Kirovskaya, is one of the deepest stations in Moscow and during World War II, the underground chambers were used by the Soviet General Command and also by the government's news service. No. 44 is described by Muscovites as the House of Three Composers. In 1843, Franz Liszt lived here when he was working in Moscow; in 1880, when the house belonged to von Meck, Tchaikovsky was a frequent visitor and the young Debussy also stayed here when he was teaching music to von Meck's daughter.

A new road, Prospekt Sakhorova was built at the beginning of the 1980s to the north of Myasnitskaya Ulitsa. It links Turgenevskaya Ploschad with Konsomolskaya Ploschad, where three main-line stations are situated. Number 39, at the end of Myasnitskaya Street, was built by the Swiss architect Le Corbusier between 1929–36 and was originally intended as the headquarters of the trade union organisation, but it now houses the government statistics office. The facade of the building faces Novokirovsky Prospekt and although it is more than 60 years old, it still looks a more modern structure and is certainly more impressive than many of the office blocks built during the late 80s. The new buildings on Prospekt Andreya Sakharova include the **Bank for External Trade**, the International Bank for Economic Co-operation and the Alfa-bank, an international finance company.

To the right of Myasnitskaya Ulitsa lies a quiet and peaceful residential quarter with several mansions dating from feudal times. One such house belonged to Prince Yusupov, where Alexander Pushkin is said to have spent three happy years of his youth.

The Bank for External Trade

Route 5

West and southwest of the Kremlin

The following section covers the area between Ulitsa Vozdvizhenka and Ulitsa Ostozhenka.

★**Ulitsa Vozdvizhenka** starts by the Russian State Library and the section from there to Arbat Square contains some interesting houses. Dating from the 17th century, the palace at No. 5 houses the Museum of Russian Architecture, which has now reopened. **The House of Friendship with the Peoples of Other Lands ❸** at No. 16 Ulitsa Vozdvizhenka is the centre for the Soviet (now Russian) Society for External Cultural Links. The lecture hall and exhibition room are used for receptions for foreign tourists, diplomats and artists. The building was constructed in Moorish-Castilian style in 1890 by the wealthy Moscow businessman Morozov.

The House of Friendship

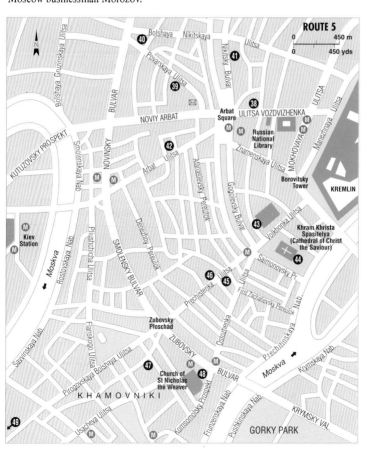

Busker in Arbat Square

The Church of
St Simeon of the Pillar

Parallel to Bozdvizhenka Ulitsa Znamenka is a fairly new museum – the Moscow State Art Gallery of Aleksandr Shilov (daily 11am–6pm, closed Monday) – which displays a selection of lovely portraits in a realist style presented to the city by local artist Shilov.

Across Arbatskaya Ploschad (Arbat Square) is Noviy Arbat (New Arbat) and a more modern part of this radial route. Eighty metres (250ft) wide and 1km (1,100yds) in length, it was designed and built between 1963–8 by a team of architects under the leadership of Posokhin. Around Arbatskaya Ploschad is a number of well known eating houses: the Praga serves Czech and Russian specialities and the Arbat near the Garden Ring is an evening venue for concerts and variety shows. Also on the Noviy Arbat is Zhiguli (Novy Arbat 11, tel: 291 4144), a restaurant designed in Soviet style. The prices are, however, decidedly Russian.

The only reminder of earlier years in this street of glass, concrete and steel is the carefully restored 17th-century **Church of St Simeon of the Pillar**. This now houses a permanent exhibition by the All Russian Society for Nature Conservancy. Noviy Arbat is one of the best areas of Moscow to look for souvenirs.

Arbatskaya Ploschad is situated at the point where the Boulevard Ring meets the end of Ulitsa Vozdvizhenka and, a little beyond the square, Ulitsa Povorskaya forks off to the northeast. It is a street which enjoyed prosperity during the 19th century and its many fine mansions now house foreign embassies. No. 25, which was built in 1820 by Giliardi as a stud farm for Prince Gagarin, is now the Institute for World Literature and also the **Gorky Museum** ❸❾ (Muzey Gorkovo; Wednesday and Friday noon–7pm, Thursday, Saturday and Sunday 10am–5pm; closed Monday, Tuesday and last Thursday in the month). Manuscripts

The Gorky Museum

and first editions of works by the founder of Russian Socialist Realism are kept here. Born Alexei Maximovich Peshkov, he was known as Maxim Gorky from 1868 until his death in 1936. After an unhappy childhood, he worked in a number of trades before devoting his life to literature. His novels which always contained elements of strong social criticism enjoyed success from the outset. In 1905, he was arrested and held in the Peter and Paul fortress in St Petersburg but, in response to public pressure, he was released. He took refuge in Capri in Italy, where he was visited by Lenin. Gorky took part in the 1917 Revolution but went back to Capri in 1921. In 1927, he returned to Russia to spend the rest of his life writing educational literature. He died on 18 June 1936.

Russian Writers' Association HQ

On the right-hand side of Ulitsa Povorskaya at No. 52, stands an early 19th-century mansion which houses the **Russian Writers' Association** ④. Well maintained and almost unaltered, it was built for Prince Dolgorukiy. Mentioned in Tolstoy's *War and Peace* as the house where the Rostov family lived, a statue of Tolstoy graces the gardens in front.

Arbatskaya Ploschad (Arbat Square) has undergone many changes since the 1960s. It is an area where many famous Russians, including Pushkin and Tchaikovsky, had their homes. Gogol also lived in this quarter of the city and two memorials to him can be seen: one is on the south side of the square and the other is in the courtyard of the house at No. 7 Nikitsky Bulvar, which runs north from Arbatskaya Ploschad.

49

Number 8a on the right side of the boulevard is a delightful villa, which is now the House of the Press, the headquarters of the Union of Moscow Journalists. No. 12, the former Lunin Palace, has become the **Museum of Oriental Art and Culture** ④ (Muzey Iskusstva Narodov Vostoka; Tuesday to Sunday 11am–8pm, last tickets 1 hour before closing). The building, which was designed by Giliardi in the Russian Empire style and was constructed in 1823, now contains important collections by artists from Japan, China, India and other eastern countries. *Objets d'art* from the Caucasus, Central Asia and the former eastern Soviet republics are also on display here.

The Museum of Oriental Art

Arbat Ulitsa is another of the main roads that meet at Arbatskaya Ploschad. It too was very popular with Moscow's art and literary world. Writers Alexander Pushkin, Leo Tolstoy, Alexander Blok and the painter Ilya Repin all lived nearby. Restored in 19th-century style, Arbata Ulitsa is a pedestrianised shopping street and it is well worth a detour as it is a popular haunt for singers, musicians and painters eager to display their talents.

At No. 26 is the **Vakhtangov Theatre** ④, which was founded in 1921 by one of Stanislavsky's pupils, Vakhtan-

The Vakhtangov Theatre

Pushkin's House Museum

Scythian exhibit in the Pushkin Museum of Fine Arts

The exterior of the museum

gov, and it specialises in modern drama. At No. 42 is the Georgian Trade and Culture Centre. Opened in 1987, there are exhibitions of paintings by Georgian artists. Georgian specialities may be sampled here (book first), and original Georgian souvenirs can be purchased. No. 55 was occupied by Pushkin for three months after his marriage in 1831. It is now **Pushkin's House Museum on the Arbat** (Kvartira Pushkina na Arbate; Tuesday to Saturday 11am–7pm, Sunday 11am–6pm, last tickets 1 hour before closing; closed Monday and the last Friday of the month). The exhibits in the rooms on the lower floor document the writer's life and work in Moscow and on the upper floor his flat has been reconstructed.

Opposite the Kremlin's Borovitsky Tower, **Ulitsa Volkhonka** heads southwest. No. 12 is the ★★**Pushkin Fine Arts Museum** ➍➌ (Muzey Izobrazitelnikh Iskusstv imeni Pushkina; Tuesday–Sunday 10am–7pm, last tickets 1 hour before closing). Designed in Classical style with white marble pillars, the museum was built between 1894–1912. Originally, Tsvetayev, a professor of art history at Moscow University, wanted the building to display casts and copies of European sculpture, but from the outset it was also used to display a collection of original paintings. From 1917, nationalised private collections were displayed to the public here, including the Rumiantsev collection and items confiscated from the tsar and aristocrats who had fled the country.

Art from ancient civilisations is displayed on the ground floor, with the exhibits originating from Urartu in Armenia, the Nile valley, the Scythia region around the Black Sea, Babylon and Greek and Roman settlements. Another downstairs room is devoted to the Italian Renaissance. The work of many French Rococo painters such as Boucher, Watteau, Poussin and Fragonard, not to mention Impressionists such as Cézanne, Ingres, Renoir, Monet, Degas and Gauguin, is displayed. Spanish artists represented here include El Greco, Murillo, Ribera and Zurbaran. Other European artists include van Dyck, Jordaens, Rembrandt, Brueghel and Cranach.

On the left-hand side at the end of Ulitsa Volkhonka is the site of the ★ ★ **Cathedral of Christ the Redeemer** , the original of which was blown up by Stalin in 1931. Until its closure in 1993, the space was taken up by the Moscow open-air swimming pool. It has now been rebuilt, its opening ceremony taking place during Russian Christmas on 6 January 2000 .

At No. 16 Ulitsa Volkhonka is a building erected at the beginning of the 19th century, Moscow's first Grammar School.

Ulitsa Prechistenka

Beyond the Boulevard Ring, Ulitsa Volkhonka becomes Ulitsa Prechistenka and there is a left fork into Ulitsa Ostozhenka. **Ulitsa Prechistenka** is one of Moscow's most elegant streets with a number of well-maintained mansions and grand residences which were built by the aristocracy. The road itself dates back to the 16th century when it served as the main route from the Kremlin to the New Maiden Convent.

51

On the left-hand side in front of a 17th-century boyar town house stands a memorial to Friedrich Engels, which was unveiled in 1976. Another fine building at No. 11 houses the ★ **Tolstoy Museum**  (Muzey Tolstovo; Tuesday–Sunday 11am–5pm, closed the last Friday of each month). Manuscripts, books, photographs, paintings and papers document the life of Leo Tolstoy, one of Russia's most revered writers, best known in western Europe for *Anna Karenina* and *War and Peace*. There is also an exhibition hall (Pyatnitskaya 12; Wednesday–Sunday 11am–5pm), which holds temporary exhibitions on Tolstoy's life. On Wednesday and Friday, the museum stages concerts.

Tolstoy plaque

On the right, at No. 12 is the ★ **Pushkin Memorial Museum**  (Tuesday–Sunday 10am–6pm, last tickets 5.30pm; closed Monday and the last Friday of the month), which should not be confused with the Pushkin Fine Arts Museum *(see page 50)*.

This fine building, which is set back from the road by a tall portico with six columns, was built in 1814 by Giliardi. The Pushkin Memorial Museum moved here in 1961. As well as memorabilia and the personal possessions of the great Russian poet, the salon is very tastefully furnished. Other rooms pay homage to the man who is often described as the 'sun of Russian literature'. The House of Scholars and Scientists at No. 16 is the place where Moscow's scientists and researchers meet to compare notes and exchange views.

No. 22 has been the headquarters of the Moscow fire brigade for almost 200 years. Nos 19 and 21 on the left-hand side are two mansions which belonged to Prince Dolgorukiy.

The Academy of the Arts

Institute for Foreign Languages, with detail

The former is now the **Academy of the Arts** and the latter is the Institute for Art History, where exhibitions of paintings by Russian and foreign artists are held from time to time.

At No. 13 Ulitsa Ostozhenka, which runs to the south of Ulitsa Prechistenka, the gate chapel of the late 17th century Zachatyevsky Convent is visible. The convent was founded in 1584 by the last member of the Rurik dynasty, the Tsar Fyodor Ivanovich, son of Ivan the Terrible.

No. 38 is another interesting 18th-century building. It was built by Kazakov in Classical style for Moscow's Governor, Yeropkin, a favourite of Catherine the Great. It is now the **Moscow Institute for Foreign Languages** and is named after Maurice Thorez (1900–64), a French communist politician.

The other side of the Garden Ring beyond Zubovskaya Ploschad, Ulitsa Prechistenka becomes Bolshaya Pirogovskaya Ulitsa. The second turning on the left is Ulitsa Tolstovo which leads to ★ **Tolstoy's House** ❹ (Dom Tolstovo; summer 10am–5pm, winter 10am–4pm, closed Monday and the last Friday of each month). It was here that the writer spent the winter months between 1882–1901 and where he wrote two of his best known works *The Kreutzer Sonata* and *Resurrection*. The house and furniture are just as Tolstoy left them: his bicycle and training weights are casually left outside the door of his study, as if he's just popped out for a few minutes.

Between Bolshaya Pirogovskaya Ulitsa and the river is an old quarter of Moscow called Chamovniki, which is an old Russian expression meaning 'weaver'. The ★ **Church of St Nicholas of the Weavers** ❹ (Tserkov Nikoly v Chamovnikach) stands at the heart of the district. This working church was built at the end of the 17th century and could well be from a Russian fairytale with its five domes, an exterior in green, gold and red, *kokoshnik* gables

St Nicholas of the Weavers

and belltower. Inside, naive paintings in the traditional colours of green and orange on a white background give a unique feel to this beautiful church.

Return to Bolshaya Pirogovskaya Ulitsa, turn left and there stands the ★★★ **Novodevichy (New Maiden) Convent ㊾** (grounds and exhibitions: Wednesday–Monday 10am–5.30pm, last tickets 1 hour before closing; the cemetery: Wednesday to Saturday 11am–4pm).

Novodevichy Convent

After the Kremlin, this convent was the second most important religious centre. One of six defensive monasteries protecting Moscow from the south and east, it is one of the finest of Moscow's sacred buildings.

The huge brick wall with its 12 towers surrounds the Cathedral of the Smolensk Icon of the Mother of God (Sobor Smolenskoy Bogomatery), four other churches, numerous convent buildings and a cemetery. Built in 1524 as a convent and fortification by Grand Prince Vasily III to commemorate the capture of Smolensk in 1514, it served to defend Moscow from attacking armies such as that of the Tartar Khan in 1551 and of the Hetmann Lithuanians in 1612.

Fortifications around the convent

The history of the convent has always been closely linked with the history of Russia. With the end of the Rurik dynasty, it was here that Boris Godunov was chosen as the new tsar in 1598; in 1689, Sofiya Alexeevna withdrew here when her half-brother Peter the Great seized power and, in 1812, the Icon of the Mother of God was taken to the battlefront where Kutuzov faced the might of Napoleon's army at Borodino.

Today, the Novodevichy Convent is a branch of the Historical Museum and the interior of the cathedral is used as an exhibition centre. In addition, documents, sacred objects, icons and the tomb of the Regent Sofiya Alexeyevna are on display.

Other parts of the complex which are of interest include the chambers of the Tsarina Irina Godunov, the 18th-century baroque belltower, the Trapeznaya church and the cemetery to the southwest, outside the walls. The convent grounds can be visited free of charge, but tickets must be bought to visit the exhibitions in the cathedral and to visit the cemetery. The remains of many cultural, literary and political figures are buried here, including Chekhov, Alexey, Tolstoy, Gogol, Skriabin, Rubinstein, Shostakovich, Shalyapin (brought from France in 1985), Khrushchev, Gromyko and Sakharov.

At the end of Bolshaya Pirogovskaya Ulitsa, inside a sharp bend in the Moskva, is a 180 hectare (450 acre) sports complex and the **Central Stadium Luzhniky ㊿**. It was built in the mid-1950s by a team of architects. This stadium can provide seating for 100,000 spectators. It is the venue for international football matches, domestic Russian competitions and many other sporting events, as well as pop concerts . Underneath the stands are indoor stadia, cinemas, a hotel and a restaurant. Other facilities

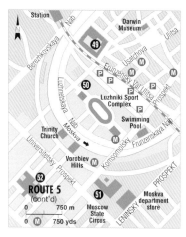

Monument outside the Palace of Children's Creativity

Moscow University

Founder Mikhail Lomonosov

include a swimming pool with seating for 13,000, the Palace of Sport which can seat 17,000 and is designed for a variety of sports such as ice-skating, ice-hockey and tennis, another smaller arena for 10,000 spectators, a youth stadium, and tennis courts. The whole complex was completely renovated and extended for the 1980 Olympic Games.

Continue out of the city towards the southwest and cross the river at the end of Komsomolsky Prospekt, which is an extension of Ulitsa Ostozhenka. On the other side of the bridge, this busy arterial road is known as the Vernadsky Prospekt. On the left stands the **Palace of Children's Creativity ⓿**. This extensive complex of glass, concrete and aluminium is connected by passageways. Built in 1962 for the Young Pioneers, the Soviet organisation for youngsters aged between 10 and 14, it now welcomes all children who want to develop their creative skills, offering workshops, laboratories, sports facilities, chess rooms, photography and film shows as well as libraries and theatres.

By the Universitet Metro station on Vernadsky Prospekt are two important cultural venues: the Moscow Central Music Theatre for Children and the Moscow State Circus. On the right is the campus of the ★**Moscow State University ⓿** (MGU), on the Vorobiev (Sparrow) Hills. These slopes are the highest in Moscow (200m/620ft above sea-level and 80m/250ft above the Moskva). The 31-storey central section of the university, which was built by a group of architects under Rudneov in 1949, is 240m (790ft) high. The four residential wings each have 17 storeys.

The university has 148 lecture rooms, a Great Hall with 1,500 seats, countless laboratories, 6,000 apartments for students and teaching staff, children's nurseries, gardens, shopping centres, a hospital, clubs, reading rooms, several museums, a library with more than a million volumes, an international theatre and a sports hall. Some of the arts faculties have stayed put in older premises in the city centre, but all science departments have moved to the new campus: physics, biology, chemistry, geography, geology, earth science and applied mathematics; as well as arts faculties such as philosophy, philology, history and law. The university grounds extend southwest from the banks of the Moskva. A monument to the founder of the university, the academic Mikhail Lomonosov (1711–65), after whom MGU is named, stands in front of the main block.

The terrace in front of the university offers a fine panoramic view over Moscow. On the right is the ski-jump and on the left the tiny Trinity Church (Tserkov Troitsy).

Route 6

South of the Kremlin

Just before the curve of the River Moskva passes in front of the Kremlin, a relief canal, built at the end of the 18th century, forks off to the northeast. It then rejoins the main flow of the river before the Novospassky Most. The island that was created by the construction of this canal is reached by four bridges from the north and four from the south. The most westerly of these bridges, the **Kamenny Most** (Stone Bridge) stands at the southwest tip of the Kremlin and was built in 1938. It provides a splendid view over the Kremlin.

The view from Kamenny Most

Nearby, a Manizer's statue of the painter Repin stands in an attractive garden with neatly-tended flower beds and fountains. It was in this quiet square, which was formerly known as Bolotnaya (Marshy) Ploschad, that the 1785 uprisings by the serfs and cossacks against Catherine the Great ended. The leader Pugachov was brought here in an iron cage and executed.

A little further to the east is **Moskvoretsky Most** (Moskvoretsky Bridge) and Ordynka Bolshaya Ordynka, which since 1937 have linked Red Square with south Moscow and beyond. On the south bank of the island are two older hotels which were renovated in 1990: the Bucharest and the Balchug. Moskvoretsky Bridge also affords a fine view of the Kremlin and St Basil's Cathedral *(see Routes 1 and 2 on pages 16 and 27 respectively)*, the Church of the Conception of St Anne (Tserkov Zatshatiya Anny) and a huge building which was once the city's main orphanage.

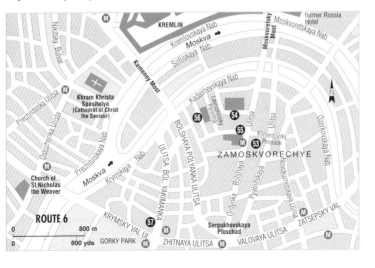

Residents of Zamoskvorechye

This is also the best place to view the remnants of the former **Russia Hotel**. Once one of the city's most memorable landmarks (and best budget accommodation options), its destruction has been a controversial and drawn-out process. Designed and built by a team of architects under Shetshulin in 1967, it was the biggest hotel in Europe with over 3,000 rooms and enough beds to accomodate over 6,000 guests. Where these buget-minded visitors will now find a room in the city centre is a main worry of local travel agents. Nevertheless, the hotel has been sacrificed to make room for more shops. The new development has yet to set a completion date, but hopes to recreate the winding streets lined with shopping and housing that were destroyed in the sixties to make room for the Rossia.

The district of Moscow to the south of the Moskva canal is called **Zamoskvorechye** (the other side of the Moskva) and in the early years of the 19th century was an area popular with traders and artisans. Both Gogol (1809–52) and Ostrovsky (1823–86) used it as the setting for their plays. In earlier times, the trade routes to the south, to the Crimea and to Astrakhan passed through this quarter. The right bank of the Moskva consequently became a settlement for merchants who supplied the Kremlin. In the 16th century, the *streltsi*, the tsar's bodyguards, also settled here, followed by manual workers and those who hoped to make a better living by serving their royal masters. By the 19th century, Zamoskvorechye was a well-to-do area occupied by merchants and the bourgeoisie, but the construction of factories later that century changed the character of the district. The workers needed to be near their workplace and ever since the needs of industry have dominated the locality. Most of the places of interest are situated between Ulitsa Pyatnitsky and Polyanka Bolshaya Ulitsa, both of which lead south from the canal and then meet at Serpukhovskaya Ploschad.

There are still one or two traces of 18th- and 19th-century life around Pyatnitskaya Ulitsa. At the corner with Klimentovsky Pereulok stands the **Church of St Clement the Pope 53** (Tserkov Svyatogo Klimenta). This late Moscow Baroque church was built in the 1760s during the first few years of Catherine the Great's reign. Side streets nearby also contain examples of churches which were built around this time, such as the Church of the Archangel Michael. Number 9 Ulitsa Malaya Ordynka was the birthplace of playwright Alexander Ostrovsky and it now houses a museum dedicated to the Russian satirist.

Bolshaya Ordynka Ulitsa (Bolshaya Ordynka Street) or the Street of the Golden Horde was the starting point of the southern trade route. Many interesting churches line this busy arterial road or are hidden away in the nearby side streets. The **Resurrection Church at Kadishi 54** (Tserkov Voskresenija Kadashakh) is a fine example of

The Virgin of All Sorrows Church

Russian Baroque. Built in 1652 by Shurchaninov, the bell-tower was added in 1695. The **Virgin of All Sorrows Church** ⑮ (Tserkov Vsyekh Skorbyashchich) was originally a Classical design by Bazhenov (1780), but was restored by Bove in 1833.

Turn right at the south end of Moskvoretsky Most and take the second turning on the left (Lavrushinsky Pereulok), which leads to the ★★★ **Tretiakov Gallery** ⑯ (Tretyakovskaya Galereya; daily 10am–7.30pm, last tickets 6.30pm, closed Monday). Housed in an old-Russian style boyar mansion with a facade designed by the painter Vasnetsov, this gallery, which was founded by the collector and art patron Pavel Tretiakov and his brother Sergei, has become the outstanding museum of Russian and Soviet art.

The Tretiakov Gallery

From fairly modest beginnings, the Tretiakov now houses a huge collection of works of art, including sculptures, copper-plate engravings, etchings and paintings. The gallery documents the history of Russian art from the 12th century to the present day. Its collection of icons is regarded as the best in the world. Andrei Rublev's celebrated *Trinity* was brought here from the monastery at Sergyev Posad. *The Virgin of Vladimir*, a unique example of Byzantine 12th-century art (now being restored), the 14th-century *Annunciation* and the 15th-century *St George* are the gallery's most valuable and prized possessions.

The Virgin of Vladimir

57

As well as 17th- and 18th-century portraits, historical paintings from the last century are prominently displayed: Karl Bryullov's *Last Days of Pompeii*, Ivanov's *The Coming of Christ*, Surikov's *Morning of the Execution of the Streltsi* and *Boyarina Morozova*.

Other notable Russian works include Levitan's delicate landscapes, Shishkin's epic forest scenes and Perov and

Ivan Shishkin:
Russian Legendary Heroes

Repin: The Religious Procession

Fedotov's witty genre scenes incorporating satire and social criticism. Repin (1844–1930) is regarded as one of Russia's finest 19th-century painters and works displayed here include *Portrait of the Composer Modest Mussorgsky, Barge Haulers on the Volga* and *The Zaporozhian Cossacks Writing to the Turkish Sultan*.

The Soviet era is characterised by numerous works depicting the civil war, the workers' environment and the Great Fatherland War (1941–5). The artist's sketches and preliminary drawings also frequently accompany the paintings.

Soviet and post-Soviet art is housed in the **New Tretiakov Gallery** (10 Krymsky Val; Tuesday–Sunday 10am–7.30pm). The sculpture garden contains statues of Communist figures pulled down after the 1991 coup. The Old Tretiakov Gallery, in which is housed an icon room and a display of 19th-century art, has reopened after undergoing extensive restoration work.

At No. 29 Polyanka Bolshaya Ulitsa stands **St Gregory's Church** (Tserkov Svyatogo Grigoriya), which was built between 1667–9. This pillarless five-domed church with its pyramid-shaped belltower and ceramic decorations is a fine example of 17th-century architecture.

Church of St John the Warrior

An unusual 19th-century building stands at No. 43 Bolshaya Yakimanka. It was designed by Pozdneyev in a highly ornate old-Russian style for a rich merchant by the name of Igumnov. At No. 46 opposite is the ★ **Church of St John the Warrior** ❺ (Tserkov Ivana Voina), which was built in 1773, combining Classical and baroque styles. The iconostasis in this working church originates from the Resurrection Church at Kadishi. At Nos 54–58 is Moscow's biggest antique and craft shop as well as a gallery which sells work by the Russian Artists' Club.

Route 7

The Sadovoye Koltso (Garden Ring)

The Kremlin is surrounded by two ring roads. The inner ring road is the horseshoe-shaped Boulevard Ring, which surrounds the city centre north of the Moskva. The outer ring road, known as Sadovoye Ring, completely encircles the city. It was constructed in the 19th century along the course of the 16th-century fortifications. Sadovaya means garden and refers to the land which remained when the old fortifications were demolished. At the beginning of the 20th century, what remained of the gardens was swallowed up by this eight to twelve lane highway. The Sadovoye Ring crosses 12 squares and consists of 17 sections, each of which has a different name.

This route describes those sights which are either adjacent or very close to the ring road. The full circuit is 15.6km (10 miles) without detours, and the best way to complete it is with a hire car and a guide, though it may be more convenient to hire a taxi. The circular trolley-bus route is also another possibility.

The best way to see the Ring

The route starts at **Kudrinskaya Ploschad** ⑤⑧, the square at the end of Ulitsa Bolshaya Nikitskaya *(see Route 4, page 39),* and continues in a clockwise direction around the Garden Ring.

At No. 6 Sadovaya Kudrinskaya is the ✱ **Anton Chekhov Museum** ⑤⑨ (Dom Chekhova; Tuesday, Thursday, Saturday and Sunday 11am–6pm, Wednesday and Friday 2pm–8pm, closed Monday and the last day of the month). Housed in a small rural-style house, where Chekhov (1860–1904) himself lived from 1886–90, this collection documents the celebrated writer's life and works from his short medical career to his literary achievements. Also on view here are portraits of Chekhov and some of his contemporaries, his writing table, his bedroom which remains unaltered and some of his manuscripts including extracts from *The Seagull* and *The Three Sisters.* There are also accounts of his journeys to Venice, Nice and Biarritz, correspondence with friends and diaries of the days spent in Melichovo, a nearby village where he lived between 1892–9.

Tverskaya Ulitsa crosses the Sadovoye Ring at ✱ **Triumfalnaya Ploschad** ⑥⓪ (Triumph Square). In 1959 a monument to the writer Vladimir Mayakovsky (1893–1930) was unveiled here. It is the second most important area for theatres after Teatralnaya Ploschad *(see Route 3).* The Tchaikovsky Concert Hall, the Satirical Theatre and the Mossoviet are all situated on this square.

Statue of Vladimir Mayakovsky

Two kilometres (1 mile) from the end of Tverskaya Ulitsa is the **Belorussian Station** ⑥① (Bielorussky Vokzal), the terminus for trains from western Europe. On the concourse is Vera Mukhina's monument to Maxim Gorky. Facing the monument, to your right, is Moscow-Berlin (Ploschad Zastava 52, tel: 251 2282), a 24-hour cosy café/restaurant with good but unobtrusive DJs.

The Belorussian Station

Northeast of Ploschad Mayakovskovo at No. 4 Ulitsa Fadeyev, which runs parallel to Tverskaya Ulitsa, is the **Central Glinka Museum of Musical Culture** (Tsentralny Muzey Muzykalnoy Kulturi imeni Glinka; Tuesday–Sunday 11am– 7pm, closed the last day of the month).

Visitors to this modern structure, which imitates a *zvonnitsa* (an old Russian belltower with several floors of open bells), can get a feel for life in Moscow's musical circles and also come to appreciate the contribution of Muscovite musicians to Russian traditions. The museum contains a number of exhibits which are associated with the life and achievements of well known Russian and west European composers and there is also an extensive collection of musical instruments and recordings. The concert hall is often used for organ recitals.

Malaya Dmitrovka Ulitsa branches off to the right towards Pushkinskaya Ploschad *(see Route 4, page 34)*. The elegant old merchants' clubroom at No. 6 is now the home of the Lenin Komsomol Theatre, better known as the LenKom.

At the junction of the Garden Ring and Karetny Ryad, Delegatskaya Ulitsa leads off to the northeast. No. 3, one of the first houses on the left, is an impressive manor house with a parade ground. This villa, built by Kazakov in the 17th century, once belonged to Count Ostermann-Tolstoy, who played an important part in the war against Napoleon. It now houses the **All Russian Museum of Decorative and Applied Art** (Vserossisky Muzey Dekorativnogo i Prikladnogo Iskusstva; open Saturday–Thursday 10am–6pm, last tickets 5.30pm, closed last Thursday of the month) and gives an insight into both traditional and modern Russian art forms.

Follow Delegatskaya Ulitsa northeast to reach **Suvorovskaya Ploschad** ❷ (Suvorov Square). As with so many parts of Moscow, this square has known many names during its lifetime. It was originally called Catherine II Square, and during Soviet times carried the title of Commune Square after the Paris Commune of 1871. On one side of the square is the Central Soviet Army Theatre (Tsentralny Teatr Sovyetskoy Armii) built in 1940 by Simburtsev and Alabyan in the shape of a five-pointed star. These days it is called the Central Russian Army Theatre. In the centre of the square stands a monument to Suvorov, by the sculptor Komov.

On the north side of Suvorovskaya Ploschad in premises built in 1821 by Giliardi as an institute for the unmarried daughters of noblemen, stands the House of the Russian Army. No. 2 Ulitsa Sovetskoy Armii is

The Museum of Decorative and Applied Art

61

Central Armed Forces Museum

Statue of Dostoevsky

The Obraztsov Puppet Theatre

Komsomolskaya Ploschad at night

the address of the nearby ★ **Central Armed Forces Museum** (Tsentralny Muzey Vooruzhennykh Sil; Wednesday– Sunday 10am– 5pm). This museum documents the history of the Red Army with papers, paintings, sculptures, trophies and weapons. One prized exhibit is the flag which was raised above the Reichstag in Berlin on 30 April 1945.

The **Dostoevsky Museum** (Wednesday and Friday 2–7pm, summer 9pm, Thursday, Saturday and Sunday 11am–6pm, closed Monday, Tuesday and the last day of the month) is situated in Ulitsa Dostoyevskovo, which joins Suvoroskaya Ploschad from the northeast. The writer Dostoevsky spent his childhood in this former hospital, where his father worked for many years as a doctor. In 1918, a **statue to Dostoevsky** by Merkurov was unveiled in front of one of the annexes to this vast building.

A little further round the Sadovoye Ring, at No. 3 Sadovo-Samotechnaya Ulitsa, is the world-famous **Obraztsov Puppet Theatre** ③. On the other side of Kolchoznaya Square stands an impressive semicircular building in Classical style. It is the **Sklifossovsky Accident Clinic** ④, occupying Count Sheremetyev's mansion, which Nazarov and Quarenghi built at the end of the 18th century. A little further on, the modern Andrei Sakharov Prospekt crosses the Sadovoye Ring.

A 26-storey skyscraper dominates Ploschad Krasniy Vorota. This block was built in 1950 for the Ministry of Vehicle Construction ⑤. In front stands Brodsky's statue of the writer Mikhail Lermontov, who was born in this district of Moscow. To the north is ★ **Komsomolskaya Ploschad** ⑥. This busy junction is some-

times just called Station Square as three stations are situated close by: St Petersburgsky Vokzal (1851), Yaroslavsky Vokzal (1904), and Kazansky Vokzal (1926). As well as the stations, the Hotel Leningradskaya (1954) and the Moskovsky department store (1985), one of the biggest in the city, can be found around the square.

Yaroslavsky Station

To the east of Zemlyanoy Val, as the Garden Ring is known at this point, is the Gorokhovoye Polye or Pea Fields district. One of its distinguished residents was Prince Kurakin, whose mansion is now occupied by the Institute of Surveyors. Another fine residence here belonged to Prince Razumovsky. Both these buildings, which are typical examples of Classical residential architecture, are by Kazakov and date from the end of the 18th century. Another fine building which is attributed to Kazakov is the nearby Church of the Assumption (Tserkov Voznezeniya) with a huge rotunda and tall belltower. A little further along Zemlyanoy Val is a modern construction, **Kurskaya Station** (Kursky Vokzal), the terminus for lines to the east and south.

Clinic for sports injuries

63

On a hill beside the banks of the Yauza is an elegant villa, designed by Giliardi, which is now a clinic ⑱ for sports injuries. A bridge crosses the Yauza, a small tributary of the Moskva, and then becomes a subway. Running parallel to the tunnel is a street which leads directly into the triangular Taganskaya Ploschad. On the right-hand side is the popular **Teatr na Taganke** ⑲. This theatre's productions always arouse considerable interest among critics and theatre-goers.

Teatr na Taganke

Just north of Taganskaya Ploschad is a side street where the Church of St Martin the Confessor (Tserkov Martina Ispovednika) is situated. Undoubtedly an attempt to imitate London's St Paul's Cathedral, it was built to plans by Kazakov at the end of the 18th century.

Behind the huge Metro station in an alleyway between some new tower blocks, is the **Potters' Church of the Assumption** ⑳ (Tserkov Uspeniya v Goncharakh). The main features of this working church are the four star-spangled, dark blue domes surrounding a central gilded dome.

To the south of Taganskaya Ploschad, on a bank high above the Moskva stands the **New Monastery of the Saviour** ㉑ (Novospassky Monastir). Although founded by Ivan Kalita in 1340, it was not completed until over a hundred years later. There are five churches behind its attractive brick wall. Two of the most interesting features are the 78m (240ft) high belltower and the frescoes in the monastery's main church, the Cathedral of the Transfiguration of the Saviour.

The New Monastery of the Saviour

The Krasnokholmsky Most now carries the Sadovoye Ring across the Moskva at a point not far from where the

The Lenin Memorial

The 16th-century Chapel and baroque New Cathedral

relief canal rejoins the main river. On the right at 31 Bakhrushinskaya Ulitsa is the **Bakhrushin Theatre Museum** 72 (Wednesday–Monday noon–6pm, closed the last Monday in the month), which documents the last hundred years of Russian theatre.

Further round the Ring is Paveletsky Station, which from an architectural point of view is the most interesting of Moscow's main stations. Fully renovated in 1987, it is the terminus for trains from the Caspian Sea region. The Garden Ring now crosses one of the busiest junctions, Serpukhovskaya Ploschad, the site of a new department store. To the north of this square is the district of Zamoskvorechye *(see Route 6, page 55)*. Lyusinovskaya Ulitsa, which later becomes Warsaw Shosse, is the main route south to Oryol, Kharkov and Yalta.

The next major square is Kaluzhskaya Ploschad, which is dominated by one of the most impressive monuments to Lenin, the **Lenin Memorial**, still standing despite the castigation of Lenin's name. Kerbel and Fyodorov's sculpture, which was unveiled in 1985, has a group of workers, symbolising the rebellious spirit of the people, underneath a female figure representing the Revolution. A pedestal with a red granite statue of Lenin looks down on the group.

The 14km (10 mile) **Leninsky Prospekt** 73 starts at this square. The southeast corner of Gorky Park can be seen from this busy arterial road which leads to Kiev. On the left is the 17-storey Akademicheskaya Hotel and on the right are two splendid monuments to Russian Classicism: the former Golitsyn Hospital (1801) and the late 19th-century Municipal Hospital (Pervaya Gorodskaya Bolnitsa) by Bove. At No. 14 in a park set back from the road, the Presidium of the Russian Academy of Sciences occupies the majestic Alexander Mansion, which Tyurin and Mironovsky designed in the 1830s. The white colonnaded hall gives sessions of the Academy something of a ceremonial atmosphere.

About 2km (1 mile) from the beginning of Leninsky Prospekt, down a side street called Donskoy Proyezd, is the ★★ **Don Monastery** (Donskoy Monastir). This is another of the six fortified monasteries which were built to protect the city from Tartar invasion. It takes its name from the miracle-working icon of the Mother God of the Don, to which the Russians attributed their decisive victory over the Tartars in 1591. Behind the rectangular walls with its twelve towers are a small 16th-century chapel and a baroque New Cathedral which was built in the 1690s. The museum in the New Cathedral is a branch of the Shchusev Museum of Architecture.

Located only a short distance from the Monastery, the Patrice Lumumba University for foreign students was opened in 1961.

A little further south is Gagarina Ploschad, where a 40m (125ft) monument to the first first man in space, Yuri Gagarin, was unveiled in 1980. At the base of the titanium statue is a steel ball which symbolises the spaceship in which Gagarin first circled the globe.

Gagarin Square and Leninsky Prospekt have become important shopping areas for the southwestern part of the city. In the 1970s, several new hotels were built in Leninsky Prospekt including Sputnik (No. 30), Sport (No. 90) and at the far end, the 33-storey Dom Turista (No. 146) and Salyut (No. 158).

The Sadovoye Ring heads northwest from Kaluzhskaya Ploschad, passing the Warsaw Hotel (Gostinitsa Varshava), beyond which lies ★ **Gorky Park** (Park Kultury i Otdycha imeni Gorkovo). This park arose from a collection of gardens, which belonged to the aristocrats and tsars in the days before the revolution. In 1928, they were combined to create a 100 hectare (250 acre) amenity, which has more to offer than most western parks: attractions include an open-air theatre with seating for 10,000, a circus, restaurants, cafés, dance floors, cinemas, exhibition rooms and a big wheel. In the summer, there are carefully-tended flower beds and lawns and in the winter, when it freezes, the park becomes a giant ice-rink. The bright, modern building on the right opposite the main entrance to the park is the Central House of Artists and the new Tretyakov Gallery of Modern Art.

The Krimsky Most (Crimea Bridge) is the only suspension bridge over the Moskva and **Zubovskaya Ploschad** is the first junction at the western end. The building on the right, in late Moscow Classical style, was built

Gorky Park entrance

65

Krimsky Most

Flower sellers in Krimskaya Ploschad

in 1835 by Stasov and Shestakov. Adjacent is the headquarters of the Novosty Press Agency.

The modern structure at No. 17 Zubovsky Bulvar, as the Garden Ring is called here, is the Progress Publishing House and bookshop.

Smolenskaya Ploschad (Smolensk Square) is situated at the junction of the Garden Ring and Arbat Ulitsa. Looking towards the city centre, Helfreich and Minkus' skyscraper dominates the immediate vicinity. It was built in 1952 to house the **Foreign Ministry**.

Away from the city, two blocks of the impressive Belgrade Hotel dwarf all the other buildings. They stand on either side of the street which leads to Most Borodina, which was built in 1912 by Osolkov and Klein. On the left on the other side of the river is **Kiev Station** ⓻, which is the terminus for trains arriving from the Ukraine. It was designed by Röhrberg between 1912–17.

A subway leads from Smolenskaya Ploschad to Noviy Arbat. At the western end of Noviy Arbat, the Novoarbatsky Most crosses the river and then the main western approach road becomes Kutuzovsky Prospekt. Just beyond Novoarbatsky Most is the **Ukraine Hotel** ⓻ (Gostinitsa Ukraina). The 140m (450ft) tower has 1,000 rooms and several restaurants. A statue in front of the hotel remembers the Ukrainian writer and revolutionary Taras Shevchenko.

The view over the north bank of the Moskva and Krasnopresnenskaya Embankment encompasses several official buildings, including the famous 'White House', residence of the Russian government; the International Trade Centre; the skyscraper by Kudrinskaya Square and the building which resembles an opened book, the former **Comecon headquarters**, now housing the government of Moscow.

Former Comecon Headquarters and Kiev Station

Route 8

Moscow from the Moskva

In the summer (May–October), river cruises on the Moskva offer fine views of Moscow. Most start from the south quay on Danilovskaya Naberezhnaya and finish at Kiev station (or run in the opposite direction). Several operators offer tours, but Moscow River Line is the most well established (tel: 459 7150). All boats have an open topped upper deck which lets you enjoy the summer sunshine.

The Danilov Monastery

The jetty stands in the shadow of the vast walls of the fortified **Danilov Monastery**, which was built during the reign of Ivan the Terrible. The buildings were fully renovated between 1984–7, just in time for the 1988 celebrations marking the 1,000th anniversary of the arrival of Christianity in Russia, which were held here. The monastery is now the residence of the Patriarch of Moscow and All Russia of the Russian Orthodox Church.

The fortified **Simonov Monastery** dates from 1385, but only the southern section's three towers, the refectory and a few other 17th-century buildings survive.

On the right rising above the Moskva's **Krutitskaya Naberezhnaya** are the brick walls of **Krutitskoye Podvorye**. The outbuildings were once the residence of the Metropolitan Bishop of Moscow, and later became barracks where the revolutionary writer Alexander Gertsin was imprisoned before being sent into exile.

Moscow from the Moskva

A little further on, on the right, is the **New Monastery of the Saviour** (Novospassky Monastir) one of Moscow's

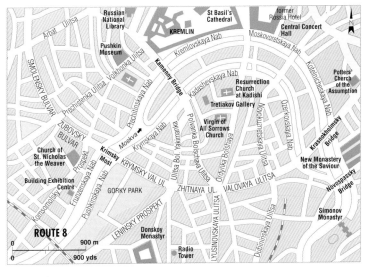

ROUTE 8

0   900 m

0   900 yds

oldest monasteries, which has just been restored. The site was endowed by Ivan Kalita in 1340 and construction began in 1446. Several churches stand within its walls. The 78m (260ft) high belltower crowned with a golden dome was added at the end of the 18th century and presents a powerful image with its galleries of columns. The five-domed **Church of the Transfiguration** (Preobrazhenskaya Tserkov) was built in traditional style between 1645–7. It is the most important of the holy places within the monastery walls and was intended to serve as a tomb for the Romanovs. Several members of the imperial family are buried here.

St Basil's Cathedral

Beyond, the **Krasnokholmsky Most**, close to the Potters' Church of the Assumption *(see Route 7, page 59)*, meets the left bank of the Moskva at the **Kosmodamianskaya Naberezhnaya Gorkovo** (Gorky Embankment), where the Institute for Technology is situated. On the right, before the mouth of the Yauza on the Kotelnicheskaya Embankment, is a huge 31-storey apartment block. Containing 700 flats, it stands over 170m (560ft) high. After **Ustinsky Most**, you might catch a glimpse of St Basil's Cathedral *(see Route 2, page 27)* and the southeast corner of the Kremlin with the Ivan the Great Bell Tower *(see Route 1, page 16)*.

After Moskvoretsky Most the cruise follows the Kremlin walls and then just beyond Kamenny Bridge *(see Route 6, page 55)* is the wall of the **Russian State Library** *(see Route 3, page 34)*. Set back from the **Bersenevsky Naberezhnaya** on the left is a 1930s tower block built which houses the Udarnik (Activist) Cinema and the New Variety Theatre.

The Russian State Library

After **Krimsky Most**, the Frunze Embankment follows the right bank of the river. The Building Exhibition Centre, which forms part of the All Russia Exhibition Centre (Usesouzny Vistivoehny Tsentr, *see Route 9, page 69*) is situated here and on the left bank opposite is **Gorky Park** *(see Route 7, page 59)*. On a hill at the far end of the park is Prince Dolgorukiy's former residence, which was built by Shchevakinsky in 1761 and redesigned in 1833 by Giliardi. A little further on, also on the left, are the buildings of the 17th- and 18th-century Andreyevsky monastery. The monastery, which was opened in the mid-17th century as Moscow's first school for 'Greek, Latin and Slavic grammar, philosophy and rhetoric', stands at the foot of the Vorobiev Hills, whose peak is crowned by the impressive 20-storey Russian Academy of Science.

As the cruise negotiates the sweeping bend of the Moskva, it passes the Luzhniki sports complex and then the walls of the **Novodevichy Convent** *(see Route 5, page 47)* before halting at the jetty near Kiev Station.

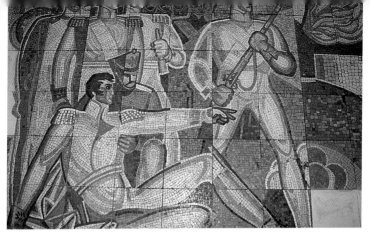

Route 9

Outlying areas

Mural outside the Borodino Panorama Museum

This section explores the sights outside the Sadovoye Ring *(see Route 7, page 59)* but inside the orbital motorway, which forms the city boundary. Situated at No. 38 Kutuzov Prospekt is the ★ **Borodino Panorama Museum** (Saturday–Thursday 10am–6pm, last tickets 4.45pm, closed the last Thursday of each month). In 1912 Franz Rubo produced an enormous painting depicting the Battle of Borodino fought against Napoleon's forces. The painting measures 115m (380ft) by 15m (50ft). In front of the museum is an equestrian statue of Field Marshal Kutuzov, which was unveiled in 1973.

Field Marshall Kutuzov

Directly opposite on Ploschad Pobyedy (Victory Square) is the **Triumphal Arch**, built between 1827–34 in honour of the Russian victory in the war of 1812. To the southwest is a memorial to the Soviet victory in the 'Great Fatherland War' (1941–5). The memorial complex includes a museum, church, synagogue and mosque, and was completed in 1995.

Over the last decade, housing estates have sprung up along Kutuzov Prospekt and in the suburb of Fili-Mazilovo to the north, so a Russian baroque building is an unusual sight in this district. The church of **Saint Mary of Fili** was built in 1693 by an uncle of Peter the Great and possesses a fine iconostasis.

Leningradsky Prospekt is one of the main approach roads to Moscow. On its right-hand side is the **Dynamo Stadium**, Moscow's second largest sports venue, with a main arena seating 60,000, and also the pseudo-Gothic **Peter Palace** (Petrovsky Zamok). This was built between 1775–82 as a royal staging post on the route to St Petersburg. The government wants to turn it into an upmarket hotel with restau-

The older generation

The Botanical Gardens

rants, bars and a dance hall. On the left-hand side is the sports complex belonging to CSKA, the Army sports club.

The **Botanical Gardens**, which were laid out by Peter the Great in 1706 as a medicinal herb garden, are at the junction of Grokholsky Pereulok and Prospekt Mira. On the left is the giant Olimpisky sports arena built for the 1980 Olympic Games. A zoo, a museum and a theatre with 200 performing animals can be found in Ulitsa Durova, which runs southwest from the sports complex, and some distance further along Prospekt Mira is **Riga Station**, a whitewashed building dating from 1899.

Beyond the railway line is the **Tserkov Troitsy**, or Holy Trinity Church, a Classical building dating from the early 19th century. Also on Prospekt Mira is the **Church of the Madonna of Tichvin in Alexeyevskoye**, an elegant church with five onion domes which originally stood in Alexeyevskoye, a village founded by Tsar Alexei Mikhailovich. By the bend in the street is the 96m (315ft) high **Sputnik Monument**. Close to Ulitsa Ostankino stands the 537m (1,780ft) high TV tower, and to the north, in the enormous grounds of Count Sheremetyev's former estate, is Ostankino Park. In 1959, part of the old estate was laid out as the ★ **Academy of Sciences Botanical Garden**. Spread over an area of 360 hectares (900 acres), it has specimens of the entire range of flora to be found throughout Russia.

Philipp the Metropolitan Church

The eastern part of the park is devoted to the ★★ **All Russia Exhibition Centre**, which often houses international trade and book fairs. Some 80 pavilions laid out over 211 hectares (500 acres) provide a complete survey of the agricultural, industrial and cultural achievements of the USSR.

Also on Prospekt Mira, underneath the monument to the Soviet space effort, near metro station VDNKH, is the **Space Museum** (Muzei Kosmosa; Prospekt Mira 111, tel: 283 7914; open Tuesday–Sunday 10am–6pm, closed last Friday of the month). Here you find old satellites, space modules and paraphernalia, and best of all, stuffed Belka and Strelka, the first dogs in space. Although Laika is more famous in the west, Belka and Strelka are better known in Russia. Laika was, indeed, the first dog in space but, unfortunately, died on reentry. Belka and Strelka were made of hardier stuff, however, and survived, hence their fame in the USSR.

Exhibits in the All Russia Exhibition Centre

A couple of minutes from the Space Museum, moving away from the metro station and past the kiosks selling bootleg/pirate DVDs and CDs, is the start of the overground **monorail** system. This is due to be opened some time in 2005. Many people have questioned the need for it, however, fearing that it will prove to be uneconomic, as tickets will cost around four times that of a metro ticket, and its route is well covered by buses, trams and trolleybuses at the moment.

In the northeast of the city is **Sokolniki Park.** Its 600 hectares (1,500 acres) of woods were once used by the

tsars for falconry. Today Muscovites share the park with touring exhibitions. Moscow's biggest church, the **Cathedral of the Epiphany at Yelokhovo** (Bogoyavlensky Patriarshy Sobor) is a work of late Russian Classicism. It was built by Tyurin between 1835–45. The iconostasis features the famous Kazan icon. Further east, at No. 3 Vtoraya Baumanskaya Ulitsa, is **Lefort Palace**, built for Admiral Franz Lefort, the Swiss-born comrade of Peter the Great. Today it houses the Archive for Military History.

On the left bank of the Yauza is the Park of Culture and Relaxation for Moscow Officers. Also in the park is the former **Annenhof Palace** (sometimes known as the Golovin or Catherine Palace), one of Moscow's finest Classical palaces. East of here is the **Church of St Peter and Paul**, built in 1711 on the orders of Peter the Great.

The Andrei Rublev Museum

Further down the Yauza is the early 15th-century Andronnikov Monastery. Originally the eastern bulwark in a system of fortified monasteries intended to protect Moscow, it now houses the ★★ **Andrei Rublev Museum** of Old Russian Culture and Art (Thursday–Tuesday 11am–6pm; closed last Friday of the month), a fine collection of icons named after Andrei Rublev, who lived there as a monk. Oddly, even though Rublev is considered to be the greatest of Russian icon painters, the collection does not include any of his work.

71

Andrei Rublev statue in Shosse Entusiastov

To the east of the museum is **Shosse Entusiastov**, which leads to Vladimir: here opponents of the tsarist regime, sentenced to exile in Siberia, began their long march east.

About 8km (5 miles) outside the city centre on the left-hand side of Shosse Entusiastov is a 1,500 hectare (3,700 acre) park, the Izmaylovo Culture Park. This was the seat of the Romanovs, the last of the tsarist dynasties. Well worth seeing are the restored lodge that once belonged to Peter I, and the Cathedral of Saint Mary, built in 1679.

About 7km (4 miles) from the city centre, along the Shosse Entusiastov in the suburb of Novye Kuzminki, is ★★ **Kuskovo Palace**, the former summer residence of the Sheremetyev family, which imitates European Rococo. The palace and park now form a museum, which has a collection of 18th-century ceramics (winter 10am–4pm, summer 10am–6pm, last tickets 1 hour before closing; closed Monday, Tuesday and last Wednesday of the month).

Kuskovo Palace

Heading south a short distance, the road forks into Kashirskoye Schosse and Varschavskoye Schosse. The old tsarist estate of ★★ **Kolomenskoye**, now an open-air museum, lies on Kashirskoye Schosse. The museum consists of many churches, some built here during the 16th and 17th centuries, and a few transported from other sites. The Church of the Ascension (Tserkov Voznyezeniya Gospodnya) commemorates the birth of Ivan the Terrible. It ranks as the most beautiful stone pyramid-roofed church in Russia.

Abramtsevo

Excursions around Moscow

There are many small towns and villages around Moscow where fine historical monuments and examples of old Russian art and architecture can be found. Unfortunately there is only room here to describe a few of the most interesting of these sights.

Abramtsevo

At the 62km (40 mile) marker on Jaroslavskoye Schosse, a road branches to the left and leads to the small estate of Abramtsevo, which in the 19th century was an important centre of Russian culture. Today the estate is a museum of literature and art (museum and grounds, Wednesday–Sunday 11am–5pm).

Early in the 19th century, Abramtsevo was owned by Sergei Aksakov, and Gogol, Turgenev, the famous actor Shchepkin and the renowned literary critic Belinsky were frequent visitors. Later in the century, the estate passed into the hands of the industrialist Savva Mamontov, a patron of many painters, sculptors and actors. The Russian artists Repin, Vasnetsov, Polenov, Vrubel, Serov and Korovin all found inspiration at Abramtsevo.

The timber house

The exhibition is laid out in a timber house with a mezzanine floor, a typical late 18th-century house design and, in fact, a considerable amount of the 18th- and 19th-century interior has been retained. There is a special room devoted to Nikolai Gogol. A valuable collection of paintings occupies six rooms and a part of the exhibition deals with Abramtsevo's own theatre, documenting the magnificent sets and costumes made to designs by Vasnyetsov, Polyenov, Vrubel and Serov.

Abramtsevo also had its own furniture workshop where carved furniture was made, and a ceramics studio in which

72

The main building at Abramtsevo

beautiful tiles, dishes and majolica were produced. The workshop today houses an interesting exhibition of crafts.

In Abramtsevo's park is a chapel built in 1882 to a design by Polenov and Vasnetsov, and the 'Hut on Chicken Legs' which was inspired by one of Vasnetsov's drawings.

The chapel

Leninskiye Gorki

By the banks of the River Pakhra, a tributary of the Moskva, lies the Gorky estate. Here the word *gorky* means hills. The estate, set in the middle of a magnificent old park, lies 35km (22 miles) southeast of Moscow, on Kashirskoye Shosse. The main building and the two smaller ones are of Classical design and date from the beginning of the 19th century.

The Gorky estate

On 25 September 1918, Lenin came here to rest and convalesce after he was wounded in an assassination attempt on 30 August. He stayed for short periods on several later occasions too, and from March 1923 until his death in January 1924, he was a permanent resident. In 1949 Gorky was opened as a Lenin Memorial (Wednesday–Monday 10am–4pm closed last Monday each month).

Everything in the house and park has been retained as it was during Lenin's day. The rooms are sparsely furnished, but there are over three thousand books. As well as Lenin's personal belongings, the museum collection includes many photos, facsimiles and other material relating to the activities of this man who, even now that the Soviet era has ended, is assured a prominent place in Russian history.

Klin

This town, lying 90km (56 miles) northwest of Moscow on the Leningradsky road, was founded in the 13th century. Reminders of the town's history and development exist in the shape of a 14th-century church and a decorative baroque church from the early 18th century.

However, the town's main attraction is the **Peter Tchaikovsky Museum** (Friday–Tuesday 10am–6pm; closed the last Monday in the month). Tchaikovsky lived in and around Klin between 1885–93. In this house, surrounded by beautiful parkland, many of the composer's scores, his library, personal belongings and letters are on view. It was here that Tchaikovsky worked on his sixth symphony, the score for *The Nutcracker*, the third concerto for piano and orchestra and 18 piano pieces.

In the adjoining concert hall, visitors can listen to first-class recordings of the composer's works. The museum also contains Tchaikovsky's piano. Twice a year, on the composer's birthday and on the anniversary of his death, leading Russian and foreign pianists pay homage to him by playing his work on this instrument.

Sergeyev Posad (1919–91 Zagorsk)

This monastery lies 71km (44 miles) northeast of Moscow city centre and can be easily reached from Yaroslavl train station, close to the Komsomolskaya metro station. The journey begins on Prospekt Mira and follows the road through villages with colourful carved *dachas*, the summerhouses inspired by the design of the peasant huts of old Russia.

St Sergius

Sergeyev Posad is an industrial town named after Saint Sergius of Radonezh who founded the monastery. For much of the 20th century it was named Zagorsk, in honour of the secretary of the Moscow Communist Party committee, Zagorsky, a native of the town, who was assassinated in 1919.

The ★★★ **Trinity St Sergius Monastery** is one of four *lavras*, the exalted Russian Orthodox monasteries. One of the others was in Kiev and this has been passed in part back to the church after serving as a museum between 1917 and 1988. The other two are the Potchayevsk Monastery in Volhynia and St Petersburg's Alexander Nevsky Monastery, which was a museum, but has reverted to its original use. The fact that these institutions were entitled to be known as *lavra* instead of *monastir* underlines their enormous importance to the spiritual life of Russia.

The monastery wall with its eleven towers surrounds seven churches, two cathedrals, a large building housing a priests' seminary and theological academy, an administration building, a former hospital and a museum for applied arts.

On the site of the first wooden church of Saint Sergius, which was plundered and set ablaze by the Tartars in 1408, a new building, the Cathedral of the Holy Trinity, was ordered by the Patriarch Nikon. It was begun in 1422, and among the artists commissioned to work on it was Andrei Rublev. In 1476, the Church of the Holy Spirit was built. At the time, the monastery was the richest landowner in all Russia, and in the early 16th century some 120,000 serfs were under its control. The Cathedral of the Assumption (Uspensky Sobor) was built on the orders of Ivan the Terrible between 1559–85, at the same time as the imperial apartments.

Little by little the hospital was completed, together with its church, dedicated to saints Zosima and Savvaty. It was followed by the refectory, built between 1686–92, then the Chapel at the Well and finally, by the gate, the Church of St John the Baptist which was completed in 1699 after six years' work.

The Holy Gate

The monastery complex is entered through the **Holy Gate** on the east side of the surrounding wall. A passage, decorated with scenes from the life of Saint Sergius, leads to the Naryshkin Baroque Church of St John the Baptist and the main courtyard. To the south is another Naryshkin

Baroque structure, the Refectory, and on the right is the Cathedral of the Assumption (*see below*), behind which stands the theological academy.

The **Church of the Holy Spirit** is now directly ahead. It was built in 1476 and was the work of architects from Pskov. In the 16th century it was altered, and only the most recent restorations have returned it to its original appearance. The arcades which serve as a belfry also form the base for the single dome.

The Cathedral of the Assumption

The ★★★ **Cathedral of the Assumption** dates from the time of Ivan the Terrible. Like the Kremlin's cathedral of the same name, it is a five-domed building. Here, however, only the central dome is gilded, the others are blue, sprinkled with gold stars. In front of the main doorway is the tomb of Tsar Boris Godunov (1598–1605) with his wife and daughter. Other points of interest are a small baroque chapel built above the holy well, an obelisk recording important episodes in the history of the monastery and the beautiful 98m (320ft) baroque belltower, designed by Rastrelli and built by Mitchurin and Ukhtomsky between 1747–61.

The oldest of the monastery's churches is the ★★ **Trinity Church**, standing some way to the left and built on the site of an earlier wooden church to Saint Sergius of Radonezh. This squat building is topped by a single dome. The attractive Chapel of Saint Nikon on its south wing is a later addition.

The ★ **Museum of Applied Art** is housed in one of the old monastery buildings, and exhibits include paintings, embroideries, religious and lay silverwork and toys, which reflect the town's importance as a toy-making centre. There are also examples of local craft and an interesting section dealing with contemporary design.

The Church of the Holy Trinity

Art and Culture

Art

Ancient Russian ecclesiastical art dates from the introduction of Christianity in 988 and was heavily influenced by Byzantine designs. At the end of the 11th century, frescoes and icons were being created, but the heyday for Moscow painters came in the 14th century, when pictures were needed for iconostases. The most important painter of this period was Andrei Rublev (his Trinity icon is housed in the Tretiakov Gallery). Towards the end of the 17th century, western influences led to the decline of traditional Russian art.

Modern Russian art owes much to Peter the Great, who summoned foreign architects and artists to his court in newly founded St Petersburg. Russian Rococo and later Russian-style Classicism were strongly influenced by Dutch architectural styles. Sculpture too was guided by European artists. Artists mainly painted portraits at this time but later on in the 19th century, historical and genre painting became a favourite theme for Russian artists. In the post-revolutionary period, many Russian artists left for western Europe, as Socialist Realism, encouraged by the Communist Party, became the only official form of self-expression. Since Perestroika, a new wave of artists has begun to fill the city's galleries.

Repin: Ivan the Terrible and his son Ivan

77

Literature

The arrival of Christianity also marked the beginnings of literary self-expression. The 12th century saw the *Chronicle of Nestor* and the *Song of Igor,* Russia's first important poetic works. The Bible was fully translated into Church Slavonic between the 15th and 17th centuries and a volume recounting the lives of Russian saints was also produced.

In the 16th century, the so-called chapbooks (popular western ballads) arrived in Russia and later, with the translation of French novels, Russian literature started to develop its own style. In the 19th century, the Russian written form was standardised by Pushkin.

Gogol, Dostoyevsky and Tolstoy wrote the first great Russian novels which explored and analysed the psychological motives of their characters, intertwining elements of social criticism. But by the turn of the century, this style had been replaced by a trend towards symbolism. In 1898, the Moscow Arts Theatre was founded by Stanislavsky and Nemirovich-Danchenko, who were responsible for publicising the works of Anton Chekhov and Maxim Gorky.

After the October Revolution, Socialist Realism preoccupied the literary world too, but many highly regarded writ-

Pushkin House Museum

Tolstoy Museum exhibit

Work by cartoonists Kurinsky, popular during World War II

ers, including Mayakovsky, Tolstoy and Sholokhov (Nobel Prize for Literature in 1965) emerged during this period. Lyric poet Boris Pasternak (1890–1960) is best known for his novel *Doctor Zhivago*, which initially was only published in the west. The book was not published in the Soviet Union until 1988. Other important Soviet writers are Mikhail Bulgakov (1891–1940) and the poets Anna Akhmatova (1889–1966) and Osip Mandelstam (1891–1938).

The period after the break up of the USSR has seen surprisingly little emerging talent. There are a few Russian writers who have broken through. One of these is Viktor Pelevin who writes twisted pop philosophy novels. His most famous books are *Chapaev and Emptiness* and *Generation P*. Another is Vladimir Sorokin who caused a scandal in the late 1990s with his novel *Golobuye Salo (Blue Lard)* which portrayed a homosexual relationship between clones of Stalin and Khrushchev. Finally, there is Tatiana Tolstoya, whose short stories, *Noch' (Night)*, have gained her wide acclaim.

Music

Russian folk music can be traced back to the 7th century with accompaniment on the balalaika and the *gusli*, a stringed instrument like the zither. An important element of Russian music is the religious chant which was first developed by Byzantine monks. In 1836, Glinka wrote the first Russian opera *A Life for the Tsar*, while at the St Petersburg Conservatory the emphasis was on west European music. Piotr Tchaikovsky, one of the greatest Russian composers, certainly wrote in the west European style, even though his music invariably took Russian themes. The most important 20th-century composers include Khachaturian (1903–78), Shostakovich (1906–75), Prokofiev (1891–1951) and the avant-garde Schedrin (b 1932).

Around the time of Perestroika, two rock groups from St Petersburg, Kino and Akvarium, became extremely popular all over the USSR. Kino split up just before the fall of the USSR when their singer Viktor Tsoi, of Korean descent, was killed in a car crash in Latvia. The group still have a fanatical following, many of whom can be seen gathering on the Stary Arbat at improvised shrines to Tsoi. Akvarium still continue to perform today, and their singer, Boris Grebenchekov, even recorded an album in English in the mid 1990s, *Radio Silence*. This is best avoided however in favour of his 'Russian' albums, *Xrectomatiya* (A Reader) being a good place to start.

In the period from 2000 to 2004, some of the most popular groups were Zemfira, girl Rock from Ufa-Pyatnitsa, a funk/reggae two piece, Umathurman, named – in one word – after the star of *Kill Bill* and other Tarantino films, and Leonid Fedyorov, whose acoustic jazz albums and concerts are well worth getting hold of/seeing.

Architecture

Most Moscow houses were made of wood until well into the 19th century; brick and stone were used in the 15th century, but only in the Kremlin's sacred buildings, although later in the noblemen's and merchants' houses. The earliest buildings display a strange blend of Byzantine forms, with oriental or Nordic (usually wooden) elements, but hardly anything in this style remains.

Between the 15th and 17th century, a style of architecture known as the Muscovite or National style emerged. Churches built at that time followed the style of churches in Vladimir, Pskov, Novgorod and other older Russian towns and are characterised by the four smaller onion domes and a larger central dome. Only in the capital is there evidence of the traditional western architecture with buildings by architects who introduced new, predominantly Renaissance styles. Many sacred buildings which date from the period after liberation from the Mongol yoke exhibit an almost exotic splendour and a wide variety of shapes and colours on top of the traditional structure. A tent-shaped tower replaced the onion domes as the church roof, but the rounded gables modelled on the *kokoshnik* (the headscarf of the Moscow housewife) were retained as the main adornment. The 17th century brought European baroque style to Russia, but Naryshkin Baroque, as it became known, was an original and impressive deviation from western European forms.

At the beginning of the 18th century, pompous decorations gave way to plainer ornamentation and the first signs of a monumental style appear. Western Classicism finally reached Russia at the end of the 18th century. The reconstruction of Moscow after the fire of 1812 was prin-

Wooden house in the Open Air Museum of Architecture

Characteristic onion domes

*Monumental style – the Foreign
Ministry building*

Post-war skyscrapers

Performance at the Bolshoi

cipally the work of Domenico Giliardi and many of the buildings from this phase are still in existence.

A more sober military or official style followed, but by the end of the 19th century it had been superseded by imitations of earlier styles such as Renaissance, Gothic, Romanesque and old-Russian Byzantine.

At the beginning of the 20th century and in the years after World War I, the influence of western art nouveau led to the construction of buildings made from concrete, steel and glass, and later to the monumental style of the 1930s.

Most of the skyscrapers and huge administrative blocks sprang up after World War II. The scale of more recent buildings has been subject to economic considerations, and also a long planning stage. Many new residential blocks were erected between 1970–5 and more new housing, along with some imaginative sports facilities, was provided when the 1980 Olympic Games complex was built. Many buildings and monuments of architectural interest were restored in the late 1980s. The work continues as churches in particular are either rebuilt or reconsecrated.

Cultural Life

Moscow is undoubtedly the home of Russian theatre. The world-famous Bolshoi Theatre (1776) for opera and ballet is just one of 50 Moscow theatres which are open from September to June. The range of music, theatre, cinema and circus on offer here probably exceeds that of any other European city. In addition to the permanent exhibitions, the city's many museums always have a wide variety of special displays. For the visitor who enjoys the arts, there can be few places more enriching than Moscow.

Music and Theatre

Most performances start at 7pm. Foreign visitors may book concert and theatre tickets at their hotel reception desk.

Concert halls

Conservatory (Great and Small Hall), Ulitsa Bolshaya 13. *Metro: Arbatskaya and Biblioteka imeni Lenina.*

Hall of Columns in the House of Trade Unions (Kolonny Zal Doma Soyuzov), Ulitsa Bolshaya Dmitrovka 1/6. *Metro: Teatralnaya Ploschad or Ploschad Revolutsii.*

Tchaikovsky Concert Hall, Ploschad Mayakovskovo 20, junction with Tverskaya Ulitsa. *Metro: Mayakovskaya.*

Theatres

Bolshoi Theatre, Teatralnaya Ploschad 2. World famous Bolshoi Theatre. Opera and ballet. Worth a visit just for the experience even if you are not a fan. *Metro: Teatralnaya/Oxotny Ryad.*

Lenkom, M. Dmitrovka Ulitsa 6. Mark Zakharov's theatre is renown for its experimental performances. *Metro: Chekovskaya.*

Maly Theatre, Teatralnaya Ploschad 1/6. Old Moscow theatre with regular performances of Russian classics. *Metro: Teatralnaya.*

Mayakovsky Theatre, Pushkarev Per 21. Theatre named after Vladimir Mayakovsky. Some good performances. *Metro: Sukhervskaya.*

Moscow Chekhov Arts Theatre (MXT), Kamergersky Per 3. World famous theatre. *Metro: Teatralnaya.*

MXAT – Gorky Arts Theatre, Tverskoi b-r 22. Respected Moscow theatre. *Metro: Tverskaya.*

Na Taganke (At Taganka), Ulitsa Zemlyanoi Val 76/21. One of Moscow's best theatres. Regularly sold out. *Metro: Taganskaya.*

Obraztova's Puppet Theatre, Sadovaya- Samotechaya Ulitsa 3. Puppet theatre. Worth a visit if you have kids. Or even if you don't. *Metro: Svetnoi Bulvar.*

Satiricon, Sheremetevskaya Ulitsa 8. Raikin's theatre. Can be hard to get tickets for. *Metro: Rizhskaya.*

Stanilavski, Tverskaya Ulitsa 23. Theatre founded by Stanislavski, author of the acting techniques used by actors all over the world. *Metro: Tverskaya.*

Theatre School of MXT's Students, Kamergersky Per 3A. Some performances in English. *Metro: Teatralnaya.*

Circuses

Circus on Prospekt Vernadskovo. *Metro: Universitet.* In the summer, the circus tent is erected in Gorky Park.

Moscow Circus of Nikulin on Tsvetnoy Bulvar (old circus). *Metro: Tsvetnoy Bulvar.*

The Bolshoi Theatre

The Mayakovsky Theatre

Food and Drink

A Russian breakfast usually consists of bread, coffee, tea, sour cream, yoghurt, milk pudding, boiled egg or omelette, hot sausages or *bitochki* (meat balls), butter or marmalade.

The main meal of the day can have three or four courses. Egg dishes, slices of meat or sausage, meat, mushroom or fish in aspic, cucumber, crab or fish salad, jellied meats, smoked fish or lumpfish may be served as an hors d'oeuvre. But other popular dishes are *shchi* (cabbage soup), *borshch* (red cabbage soup with a dash of cream and a dash of *kvas*), *botvinya* (cold smoked fish soup with radish, cucumber, onion and kvas), *rassolnik* (beef stock with vegetables and gherkins, kidneys and soured cream) and meat ball soup. Another popular starter in summer is *okroshka* (boiled meat, hard-boiled egg, finely chopped onions, fresh cucumbers and kvas served ice cold). Main courses are likely to be beef, pork, chicken, duck, game, mushrooms, fish (including salmon, sturgeon, zander and sterlet) with potatoes, beetroot, cucumber, vegetable, salad, etc.

A typical starter

Popular desserts are cakes, biscuits, ice cream, *bliny* (buckwheat pancakes with a sweet sauce), grapes or apples, puréed fruit and *kissel* (fruit juices mixed with fresh red fruit or dried fruit thickened with arrowroot and served with fresh cream).

83

Specialities from other regions of the former Soviet Union often found on menus are Chicken Kiev and *galushky* (small boiled dumplings) from the Ukraine. *Shashlik* originates from Georgia and *dolmas* (minced meat with tomatoes, paprika wrapped in vine leaves) is an Armenian dish. *Chebureki* (meat pastries) from the Crimea and *pelmeni*, a Siberian ravioli, are also available in Moscow restaurants.

Russian drinks include tea, mineral water, fruit juices, beer, vodka, dry wines from Georgia, dessert wines from the Ukraine, Armenian and Georgian cognac and sparkling wines from the Crimea. *Kvas* is a type of lemonade made from dried black bread fermented with yeast and raisins.

The local tipple

Russian vodka is world famous and the recommended brands include Stolichnaya, Russkaya, Moskovskaya Osobaya and Zolotoye Koltso. The Armenian brands of cognac are fairly mild. Russian champagne comes in four varieties: dry, medium dry, medium sweet and sweet.

Restaurants

Though dining out in Russia is a new concept, the capital has embraced it much more quickly than anywhere else. It's hard to believe that ten years ago the only choice available to visitors was between bad food in a foreign hotel and worse food in a workers' cafeteria. This still isn't a gourmand capital, but at least now there are choices with restaurants serving good Russian and European cuisine as well as Georgian, Indian and Chinese.

Out on the town

Restaurants below are organised by price based upon the cost of a meal for one. *$$$* – more than US$50, *$$* – US$20–50, *$* –less than US$20.

$$$

Oblomov, 1 Monetchikovsky Per 5, tel: 953 6828. Good Russian food. Expensive. *Metro: Novokuznetskaya.*
Red Square, 1 Red Square (Krasnaya Ploschad), tel: 925 3600. Noble Russian dishes from the 18th and 19th centuries. *Metro: Oxotny Ryad.*

$$–$$$

Tandoor, 30 Tverskaya Ulitsa, tel: 299 5925. Tasty Indian food. Good service. Good for vegetarians. *Metro: Tverskaya.*

$$

Goa, Ulitsa Myasnitskaya 8/2, tel: 504 4031. Modern restaurant with a fusion menu of Indian, Chinese and Russian cuisine. *Metro: Lubyanka.*
Mexana Bansko, 9/1 Smolenskaya Ploschad, tel: 241 3132. Tasty, filling Bulgarian food. Good atmosphere. *Metro: Smolenskaya.*

$–$$

Yama, 10 Stoleshnikov Per, tel: 292 0115. Tasty food. Nice atmosphere. Follow the smell of food and sound of music to find it. Located behind shop fronts. *Metro: Pushkinskaya.*

$

Moo Moo, 26 Komsomolskaya Prospekt, tel: 245 7820. Cheap, delicious Russian food. Can get very crowded. *Metro: Frunzenskaya.*

Tipping

McDonalds

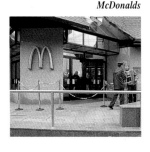

Waiters, porters, and taxi drivers, especially in Moscow and St Petersburg appreciate tips. Ten percent is the accepted rule. While in Soviet times a small gift would suffice, today Russia is a moneyed economy, so tip your guides and interpreters accordingly. They will certainly appreciate it.

Bars and nightclubs

Bilingua, Krivokoleny Per 10, tel: 923 9660. Art café, nice atmosphere. *Metro: Chistiye Prudy.*
Kitaiskii Lyotchik (Chinese Pilot), Lubyansky Per 25/12, tel: 924 5611. One of Moscow's most popular clubs. Bar, restaurant, live concerts. *Metro: Kitai Gorod.*
Pariskaya Zhizn' (Paris Life), Ulitsa Karetniy Per 3, tel: 209 4524. Straightforward Disco. *Metro: Pushkinskaya.*

Piro .G.I, Ulitsa Nikolskaya 19, tel: 921 5827. Good bar/bookshop. Very crowded at weekends. *Metro: Lubyanka.*

Propaganda, Bolshaya Zlatoustinsky Per 7, tel: 924 5732. One of Moscow's most famous clubs. Flies in DJs from Britain and America. *Metro: Kitai Gorod.*

Shestnadsat' Tonn, Ulitsa Presnensky Val 6, tel: 253 5300. Upmarket imitation British bar. Better than it sounds. Homemade beer. *Metro: 1905 Goda.*

Sport Bar, Ulitsa Novy Arbat 10, tel: 290 4311. A club with an unusual mix of live sports transmissions, concerts and sushi. *Metro: Arbatskaya.*

Trety Put', Ulitsa Pyatnitskaya 4 , tel: 951 8734. Underground club in an old *Komunalka. Metro: Novykuznetskaya.*

Vermel, Raushskaya Hab 4, tel: 959 3303. Club popular with students. Live concerts. Overlooks Red Square. *Metro: Novykuznetskaya.*

Shopping

Limited goods and opening hours are a thing of the past in Russia: there are shopping malls and food stores all over Moscow these days. Almost all of them are private enterprises, with notable exceptions such as the department store, GUM, which has a state share. Privatisation of trade has helped to improve service and many shops are open at least 12 hours per day. Some are open 24 hours.

Fresh fruit and vegetables can be bought at outdoor markets (*rynok*), but most Muscovites do their daily shopping in groceries. These have lower prices than supermarkets, but the choice of goods is usually smaller and they may have queues in rush hour. If stocking up, it is probably better to visit a supermarket where you can buy good quality imported and Russian goods.

85

The underground scene

The main shopping streets, Novy Arbat, Kuznetsky Most and Tverskaya Ulitsa, are lined with big chain shops and numerous boutiques with clothes by leading international and Russian designers.

The Arbat every day and the Vernisage at Izmailovsky Park on Saturdays and Sundays are the best known spots for souvenir shopping, and have the widest selection in one location. Souvenirs can also be found in special shops for foreigners, art salons and curio shops.

Visitors should beware of the Russian customs regulations. For goods bought in a Russian shop, you must keep the receipt as proof of purchase and to show that the goods are not antique.

Bring plenty of roubles with you. Although most supermarkets and big stores do accept credit cards some may question the safety in an area so inundated with fraud and computer hacking. If you carry dollars you are rarely caught out as bigger stores offer their own currency exchange services.

*Strolling along
the Arbat*

Shops

Department Stores
GUM, Krasnaya Ploschad 3; **TsUM**, Ulitsa Petrovka 2; **Petrovsky Passage**, Ulitsa Petrovka 10; **Detskiy Mir**, Teatralny Proyezd 2; **Moskva Department Store**, Leninsky Prospekt 54.

Boutiques
Gianni Versace, Kuznetsky Most 19; **Hugo Boss,** 1-st, Tverskaya-Yamskaya Ulitsa 13/1; **Moscow Fashion House Slava Zaitsev**, Prospekt Mira 21.

*Souvenirs outside the
Novodevichy Convent*

Antiques

Antikvar-Metropol, Teatralny Proezd 1/4, Hotel Metropol; **Arbatskaya Nakhodka**, Ulitsa Arbat 11; **Zolotoy Larets**, Ulitsa Arbat 6/2.

Books

Pangloss, Ulitsa Prichistenka 1. *Metro: Kropotkinskaya*; **Rubikon**, Kaluzhskaya Ploschad 1. In the same building as the Children's Library. *Metro: Oktyabraskaya*; **Dom Innostranoi Knigi**, Kuznetsky Most 18. *Metro: Kuznetsky Most*; **Biblio Globus**, Myasnitskaya Ulitsa 6. *Metro: Lubyanka*; **Dom Knigi on the Novy Arbat**, Ulitsa Novy Arbat 8. *Metro: Arbatskaya*.

GUM

Internet Access

Internet cafés open and close all the time, and are not particularly hard to find, especially in the centre. **Kuznetski Most Café**, Kuznetski Most 12, tel: 924 2140. Open 10am–midnight. *Metro: Kuznetski Most*; **Manezh Shopping Centre**, Manezhnaya Ploschad, tel: 363 0060. On the ground floor of the Oxotny Rad shopping complex, this is apparently the biggest Internet café in Eastern Europe. Open 24 hours. *Metro: Oxotny Riad/Teatralnaya*; **Netland**, 2 Rozhdestvenka Ulitsa, tel: 781 0923. Pool tables, table football and Internet access. *Metro: Lubyanka*; **British Council**, Nikoloyamskaya Ulitsa 1, tel: 234 0201. Located in the library. Not many computers, but you can read English newspapers whilst waiting. *Metro: Kitai Gorod.*

87

Foods

Eldorado, 1 Bolshaya Polyanka; **Global USA**, 112 Leningradskoe Schosse; **Manege Shopping Mall**, three-floor underground shopping mall directly under Manezhnaya Ploschad, accessible from Oxotny Ryad metro; **Perekriostok**, Sukharovskaya Ploschad 1; **Ramstore**, Sheremetevskaya Ulitsa 60a; **Seventh Continent**, 12 Bolshaya Lubyanka.

Vegetable stand at the Tsentralny Rynok

Jewellery

Faberge, Kuznetsky Most 20; **Samotsvety** (semi-precious stones), Ulitsa Arbat 35; **Brilianty** (diamonds), Tverskaya Ulitsa 18A; **Chopard,** Teatralny Proezd 1/4.

Farmers' Markets

Cheryomushkinsky Rynok, Lomonosovsky Prospekt l/42, **Yaroslavsky Rynok**, Prospekt Mira 122в.

Flea Markets

Izmaylovo, Izmaylovsky Prospekt 63; **Luzhniky,** Luzhnetsky Prospekt; **Konkovo Trade Complex**, Profsouznaya Ulitsa 122–130.

Getting There

By plane

There are daily flights from London Heathrow with Aeroflot and British Airways. Moscow is also served by direct flights from New York, which take nine hours. If coming from Europe, it is also possible to fly daily with Scandinavian Airlines via Stockholm, with Finnair via Helsinki, or with Lufthansa via Frankfurt. There are two main international airports in Moscow. Sheremeytovo II, an old Soviet era affair, and Domodedovo II, located in the south of the city. The latter is a new, modern airport, with an express rail link to Moscow. Domodedovo II is taking more and more business away from Sheremeytovo, and is likely to become the city's main international point in the near future.

By train

Railways connect the largest Russian cities with west European capitals and for travellers who can spare the time, there are comfortable first-class sleeping cars, which are the pride of the Russian railways, although the journey from London will take about three days. A change of gauge is necessary at the Russian border.

By car

The restrictions which applied to motorists from western Europe during the Soviet era have now been lifted and it is possible to enter from any crossing point.

The main crossing points are as follows:
Poland: Terespol–Brest. This is the quickest route to Moscow passing through Minsk and Smolensk (1,054km/630 miles); Medyka–Shegini (October–May).
Romania: Siret–Porubnoe and Albita–Leusheny.
Slovak Republic: Michalovce–Uzhgorod.
Hungary: Zahony–Chop, via Lvov, Kiev and Orel.
Finland: Vaalimaa–Torfyanovka & Nujamaa–Brusnichnoe.

Automobile associations provide further information for motorists intending to visit Russia. Hotels, motels, campsites, petrol stations and breakdown services are located at regular intervals along the main roads. Intourist and other specialists *(see page 92)* also supply information to motorists.

If you intend to continue within European Russia you can drive to the Caucasus and the Black Sea, ferrying the car across to Yalta or Odessa and crossing the Ukraine to Slovakia or Poland. Since crossing the border into Turkey is now possible, you can also exit or enter Anatolia. Whether this route remains open, however, depends on the changing political conditions in the Caucasus.

Opposite:
Leningradsky Station
Happy landings

Try the train

89

Moscow Metro

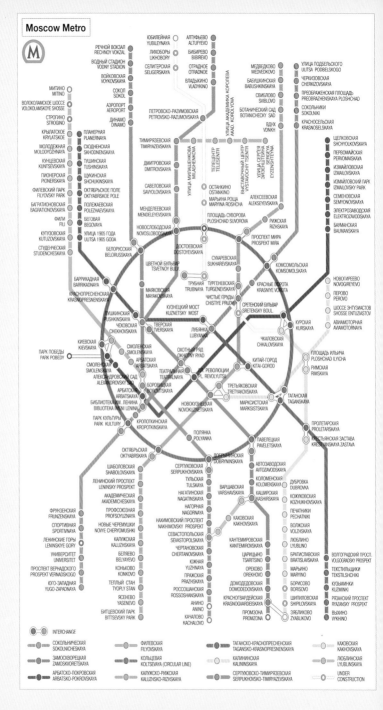

Getting Around

The Underground (Metro)

The quickest and most convenient form of transport in Moscow is the Metro, with 157 stations covering 250km (160 miles). Trains run every three minutes from 6–1am. Fares increase sharply every few months, but are still relatively cheap to foreigners. Metro cards may be bought from the ticket offices in the entry halls.

The stations are tourist attractions in their own right. These underground palaces were designed by the country's best architects using materials such as marble, bronze and glass. Famous artists are responsible for the décor.

Trams, trolleybuses, buses and taxis

The tram system services outlying districts (5.30–1am). Most maps show bus routes (and trolleybuses: 6–1am), but it is usually quicker to take the Metro.

There are two types of taxi: those for personal use (day and night) and the *marshrut* taxis, which operate one route (9am–9pm). (tel: 927 0000/923 2108, but it is probably easier to hail one). Taxis are usually yellow with a narrow chequered band round the sides and all are metered. There is no official tariff, though, and fares vary considerably. Many private car owners operate unofficial taxis.

A Metro to marvel at

River trams

Between May and September, river trams and hydrofoils ply up and down the Moskva. It is best to board at the jetty near Kiev Station and to head towards Moskvorechnaya Naberezhnaya, which is near Kotay Gorod Metro station *(see Route 8, page 67)*. The journey lasts 1½ hours.

Kiev Station embankment

Main roads

Moscow's main roads are signed by a white letter on a blue background: A–the Boulevard Ring (Bulvarnoye Koltso); B–Garden Ring (Sadovoye Koltso); K–Motorway Ring. The radial roads: M-1–Kutuzovsky Prospekt heads west towards Minsk, Brest and Warsaw; M-4–Warsaw Shosse heads south towards Kharkov, Simferopol and Yalta; M-8–Entuziastov Shosse heads northeast to Vladimir and Suzdal; M-9–Prospekt Mira to Sergiev Posad; M-10–St Petersburg Prospekt to Leningradsky. The speed limit in the left-hand lane of these and other main trunk roads is 80km/h (50mph); on all other roads, it is 60km/h (37mph).

House numbers

Unlike in the rest of Europe, apartment blocks are numbered, rather than entrance doors. On ring roads and roads which run parallel, numbers go from right to left as seen from the city centre. Even numbers are always on the right.

Facts for the Visitor

Travel documents

Visitors must have a valid passport and visa. A tourist visa is valid for one month and varies in price, depending on how quickly it is needed. The easiest way to get one is through a travel agent *(see below).*

Customs

Not for export

Antiques and manuscripts may not be exported without permission from the Russian Ministry of Culture. One person can take home up to 280 grams of caviar, 2 litres of wine, 1½ litres of spirits and 1,000 cigarettes. All valuables including watches, wedding rings, cameras and personal stereos, must be declared on arrival (to avoid problems).

Exchange regulations

Foreign currency, travellers' cheques and letters of credit may be imported, but must be declared upon arrival on a customs declaration form. Currency taken out must not exceed the amount shown on the import declaration.

92

Travel agents

In the UK:

Andrews Consulting, 31 Corsham St, 2nd floor, London N1 6DR, tel: (020) 7490 8142, London@actravel.com; **Asla Ltd**, 160 High St, Huntingdon, Cambridge PE29 3TF, tel: (0148) 043 3783, info@asla.co.uk; **Hogg Robinson Business Travel**, 12 Caxton St, London SW1H OQS, tel: (020) 7222 8711; **Russia Direct Ltd**, 39 Palmerston Place, Edinburgh, EH12 5AU, tel: (0131) 476 7727, info@russiadirect.net; **Russian Gateway UK Limited**, travel@russiangateway.co.uk.

In the US:

Russian National Group, 130 West 42nd Street, Suite 1804, New York, NY 10036, tel: (877) 221-7120/(212) 575-3431, info@rnto.org; **Peace Travel Services**, 1648 Taylor Rd #222, Port Orange, Fl 32128, visa@go-russia.com.

In Moscow:

Incentive Group Inna Travel, Ulitsa 2nd Brestskaya 39/4, tel: (095) 926 5556, www.business-travel.ru; **Visa House**, 22 Bolshaya Nikitskaya, Office 18, Moscow, tel: (095) 721 1021, www.visahouse.com.

Motorists drive at their own risk

Motoring

Cars drive on the right. Foreign motorists drive their cars at their own risk. Although there is no longer any need to submit travel plans to the authorities, diverting from the established routes is not advisable as accommodation is hard to find. It is recommended that you organise your journey through a recognised travel agency.

Details of cars must be entered on the visa. Visitors must have an international driving licence and documents verifying their right to drive the car (in Russian) obtainable from Intourist *(see page 92)*. All foreign cars must show a nationality plate.

There is no obligatory Third Party Liability and the Green Card or international insurance certificate does not apply, although at the border it is possible to obtain cover for short stays through the state insurance company Ingosstrakh, Piatnitskaya 12, Moscow, tel: 232 3211.

Currency and exchange

It is unwise to change money on the street. There are bureaux de change throughout the city, many of which can be found in hotels. You will need to present your passport when changing money. The 1994 currency regulations dictate that payment for goods and services can only be made in roubles or by credit card. Eurocheques are no longer accepted.

Roubles come in banknotes and coins. Details of exchange rates are available from all bureaux de change.

Opening times

Offices: Monday to Friday 9am–6pm; *Food shops*: Monday to Saturday 8am–1pm and 2–9pm, Sunday 8am–1pm and 2–6pm (Some open 24 hours, see *Shopping, page 85*). *Other shops*: Monday to Saturday 11am–2pm and 3–9pm. The GUM department store and other large shops: 8am–9pm.

Newspapers

The most informative newspapers are the *Moscow Times* and the *Russian Journal*, available (in English) in most hotels.

Photography

Photographic equipment is easily obtained and there are quick film-developing services. Most hotels sell photographic equipment. *Shops*: **Canon** shop, #1 Stoleshnikov Pereulok 5; **Upiter**, Ulitsa Novii Arbat,19; **Kodak**, Ulitsa Znamenka, 15 and at GUM, Krasnaya Ploschad 3.

Temples and churches

Anglican, St Andrew's, Voznesensky 9; **Catholic**, Chapel of our Lady of Hope, Kutuzovsky Prospekt 7/4, Korpus 5, Entrance 3, Floor 3, Apartment 43; **Protestant**, UPDK Hall, Ulitsa Olafa Palma 5, Korpus 2; **Synagogue**, Spasoglinischevsky Pereulok 8; **Greek Orthodox**, Arkhangelsky Pereulok 15A; **Muslim Mosque**, Vypolzov Pereulok; **Russian Orthodox** – throughout the city.

Hot dog stall

John Bull Pub, Kutuzovsky Street

Public holidays in Russia

1–5 January (New Year's Holidays); 7 January (Orthodox Christmas Day); 23 February (Army Day); 8 March (Women's Day); 1 May (May Holiday); 9 May (Victory Day); 12 June (Independence Day); 4 November (Unity Day).

Post offices, telephones and telegrams

Main post office (Glavny Pochtant), Ulitsa Myasnitskaya 26a, 8am–10pm; every large hotel has a post office with facilities for basic postal services. The address of the international post office is Warsaw Shosse 37, tel: 114 4589, 8.30am–7.30pm.

Post offices are usually open by 10am, but routine postal services are available at reception in the larger hotels between 8am–10pm. It is advisable to check charges at tourist offices.

Telephone kiosks

Central telephone office (Tsentralny Mezhdunarodny Telefonny Peregovorny), Tverskaya Ulitsa 7, entrance in Gazetny Pereulok 1. Central telegraph office (Tsentralny Telegraf), Tverskaya Ulitsa 7.

Local calls may be made from hotels at no charge, but from telephone boxes, a local call will cost a minimal amount. To make an international call, dial 8 +10 + the international code: Australia 61; France 33; Germany 49; Japan 81; Netherlands 31; Spain 34; UK 44; US and Canada 1. From abroad, dial 007 for Russia and 95 for Moscow.

Time difference

Moscow time is three hours ahead of Greenwich Mean Time. In summer the clock is put forward an hour.

Medical and other emergencies

Chemist Sign

Visitors should ensure they have enough of any drugs they are likely to need. Here are some contacts for emergencies: *Fire* 01; *Police* 02; *Ambulance* 03; *Gas leak* 04.

American Medical Center, 1 Grokholsky Pereulok, tel: 933 7700; *Russian-American Medical Centre*, 2-d Tverskoy-Yamskoy Pereulok 10, tel: 250 0646; *Athens Medical Center*, Michurinsky Prospekt 6, tel: 147 9322/ 143 2387;

European Dental Centre, Konyushkovskaya Ulitsa 34, tel: 797 6767.

Drugstore at Sadko Arcade, Krasnogvardeysky proezd 1, tel: 253 9592; *Pharmacy Central Enquiries*, tel: 927 0561.

Embassies

Australia: Kropotkinsky Pereulok 13, tel: 956 6070.
Canada: Starokonyushenny Pereulok 23, tel: 956 6666.
UK: Sofiyskaya Naberezhnaya l0, tel: 956 7200.
USA: Bolshaya Devyatinskiy Per 8, tel: 728 5000.

Accommodation

Hotels

When you check into a Russian hotel you will be given a guest card which you should carry at all times. Each hotel has a service bureau which will assist you in all small matters, from medical help to calling a taxi or obtaining theatre and concert tickets, restaurant reservations or arranging international telephone calls.

Luxury

Baltschug Kempinski Moskau, Ulitsa Baltschug 1, tel: 230 6500, www.kempinskimoscow.com, www.kempinski-moscow.ru. German chain hotel with excellent views of the river. Across from the Kremlin; **Marriott Grand Hotel**, Tverskaya Ulitsa 26, tel: 935 8500, www.marriott.com. Centrally located hotel, popular with visiting politicians; **Metropol**, Teatralnay Proyezd 1–4, tel: 927 6000, metropol@metmos.ru. One of the most luxurious hotels in Moscow. Beautiful interior.

The Metropol Hotel

Expensive

Radisson-Slavyanskaya, Berezhnaya Nab 2, tel: 941 8020, www.radissonsas.com. Luxury hotel with bars, restaurants and a cinema that shows English language films; **Sheraton Palace Hotel**, Ulitsa Tverskaya–Yamskaya 1st 19, tel: 931 9700, www.sheraton.ru. Western style hotel. Good location for sightseeing; **Sofitel Hotel Iris**, Korovinskoye Shosse 10, tel: 488 8000, www.irisreservation.ru. A good quality hotel. A long way from the centre though; **Le Meridien**, Nakhabino Moscow Country Club, tel: 926 5911, www.lemeridien-mcc.com. 30km (19 miles) from Moscow. Good rates. Good quality hotel; **Novotel**, Sheremetevyo II airport, tel: 926 5900. Airport hotel. Nothing special; **Renaissance Hotel**, Olimpysky Prospekt 18/1, tel: 931 9000/9833, businesscenter@co.ru. A luxury hotel, with an English language cinema. A little far from the centre.

The Savoy Hotel

Moderate

Akademicheskaya Hotel, Donskaya Ulitsa 1, tel: 959 8157. Ordinary hotel, nothing special. Centrally located; **Cosmos**, Prospekt Mira 150, tel: 215 6791. Reasonably priced hotel with a great location. Close to VDNKH, and the monument to the Soviet space program; **Hotel Mayak**, Bolshaya Filyovskaya 25, tel: 142 2117. Comfortable rooms, reasonably priced; **Ukraina**, Kutuzovsky Prospekt 2/1, tel: 243 2596/3030. One of Moscow's gothic wedding cake buildings. Excellent views. Good off season rates.

Budget

Belgrad, Ulitsa Smolenskaya 8, tel: 924 8820. Basic hotel, far from the centre; **Budapest**, Petrovskiye Linii 2/18, tel: 924 1643. Good downtown location; **Izmayalov**, Izmayalov 71, tel: 166 3627. Located 15 minutes by metro from the centre and next to the Izmayalovsky Arts and Craft market. English speaking staff.

Index